Pathfinder® Guides

C000274331

Lake District
West & South Lakeland

Walks

Compiled by
Terry Marsh

Text: Terry Marsh
Photography: Terry Marsh
Editorial: Ark Creative (UK) Ltd
Design: Ark Creative (UK) Ltd

This product includes mapping data licensed from Ordnance Survey® with the permission of the Controller of Her Majesty's Stationery Office. © Crown Copyright 2009. All rights reserved. Licence number 150002047. Ordnance Survey, the OS symbol and Pathfinder are registered trademarks and Explorer, Landranger and Outdoor Leisure are trademarks of the Ordnance Survey, the national mapping agency of Great Britain.

ISBN 978-1-85458-497-7

While every care has been taken to ensure the accuracy of the route directions, the publishers cannot accept responsibility for errors or omissions, or for changes in details given. The countryside is not static: hedges and fences can be removed, field boundaries can alter, footpaths can be rerouted and changes in ownership can result in the closure or diversion of some concessionary paths. Also, paths that are easy and pleasant for walking in fine conditions may become slippery, muddy and difficult in wet weather, while stepping stones across rivers and streams may become impassable.

If you find an inaccuracy in either the text or maps, please write to Crimson Publishing at the address below.

First published in Great Britain 2009 by Crimson Publishing, a division of:
Crimson Business Ltd,
Westminster House, Kew Road, Richmond, Surrey, TW9 2ND

www.totalwalking.co.uk

Printed in Singapore. 1/09

A catalogue record for this book is available from the British library.

Front cover: Coniston Water at Nibthwaite
Previous page: Tarn Beck

Contents

Approximate walk times

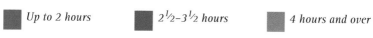

Up to 2 hours $2^{1}/_{2}$–$3^{1}/_{2}$ hours   4 hours and over

The walk times are provided as a guide only and are calculated using an average walking speed of $2^{1}/_{2}$mph (4km/h), adding one minute for each 10m (33ft) of ascent, and then rounding the result to the nearest half hour.

Keymap

WHITEHAVEN

Low
Moresby
Parton
172
247
Asby
Lamplugh
Grasmo
851

River Keekle
Arlecdon
Rowrah
16
211
Cogra
Moss
Loweswater Fell
572
CRUMMOCK
WATER

Moresby
Parks
Kirkland
Croasdale
Scale Force
511
Butter

Murton Fell
Frizington
Ennerdale
Bridge
616
Great Borne
Red Pike
806
High Stile
BUTTERMERE

CLEATOR
MOOR
Grike
ENNERDALE
WATER
Ennerdale
Fell
Pillar
892

26
Scoat Fell
841
Black

Moor
Row
Bigrigg
Clea
17
673
Caw Fell
Haycock
801

20
River Ehen
St Bees
140
290

EGREMONT
Castle
322

Coulderton
Thornhill
Halle
Seatallan
692
COPELA
FOREST

Middletown
Nethertown
Calder
Bridge
27

Beckermet
Gosforth
River Bleng
Nether
Wasdale
14
18
WAST WAT
Burn
Tar

Braystones
Works
A595
67
The Screes
337

Sellafield Sta
B5344
River Irt
12
Beckfoot

Seascale
Santon
Bridge
1

Holmrook
Gubbergill
Eskdale
Green
Stanley
Force

Drigg
30
3
River Esk
2
Devoke
Water

Kokoarrah
Ravenglass
6
Muncaster
Castle
Woodend
Ulpha Fell

ROMAN
BATH HOUSE
Broad Oak
Whitfell
573

Waberthwaite
Lane End

Stubb
Place
Corney
Prior Park

Tarn Bay
Stoneside
Hill

Hycemoor
Bootle
Station
Bootle Fell

Selker Bay
Bootle
600

Annaside
Black Combe
25
A595

Silecroft
Whicham
A5093

Kirksanton
MI

SCALE 1:208,333 or 1 inch to about 3¼ MILES *1CM to 2.1KM*
0 2 4 6 8 10 KILOMETRES 15
0 2 4 6 MILES 8 10
KEYMAP HEIGHTS SHOWN IN METRES

Haverigg

Duddo

Keymap

Causey Pike · Dowthwaitehead · Dockray · Mountain Sch
A591 · Great Dodd · Aira Force
DERWENT WATER · B5289 · Beck
Little Town · Great Dodd · 840 · Sandwick
Derwent Fells · Lodore Falls · Legburthwaite · Glenridding · 657 · Marti
Newlands Hause · Grange · 608 · High Seat · Patterdale · 27 · Beda Fell
737 · Watendlath · Bridgend · Angle Tarn
Buttermere Fell · 754 · THIRLMERE · HELVELLYN · Hartsop
Honister · Rosthwaite · 950 · Grisedale · Brothers Water
Seatoller · Stonethwaite · Wythburn Fells · Grisedale Tarn · Hayeswater · 191
Scarth Gap · Pass · Seathwaite · Borrowdale Fells · Seat Sandal · 873 · 763
Hay Stacks · 722 · Dunmail Raise · Kirkstone Pass
28 · Wrigill Force · Ullscarf · Easedale Tarn · Rydal Fell · 776 · Kirkstone Pass Inn
Kirk Fell · Gable · 899 · Glaramara · 762 · Kirkstone Pass Inn
Wasdale Head · Sty Head · High White Stones · Grasmere · Rydal Mount · A592
Lingmell · Great End · Stickle Tarn · Dungeon Ghyll Force · Rydal Water · Rydal
978 · L PIKE · 23 · Bow Fell · 902 · Langdale Pikes · Chapel Stile · 335 · 487
964 · SCA FELL · LAKE DISTRICT NATIONAL PARK · Elterwater · Little Langdale · Ambleside · Troutbe
Wrynose Pass · B5343 · Clappersgate · Waterhead · Town End
ROMAN · 21 · Hardknott Pass · Skelwith Bridge · A591 · Townend · Troutbeck Bri
Cockley Beck · River Brathay · A593 · 322 · WINDE
Birker Force · 653 · 19 · Outgate · High Wray · WINDE
Levers Water · 803 · Hawkshead · Clatte Heights · BOWNESS
Seathwaite · 10 · OLD MAN OF CONISTON · 9 · Esthwaite Water · BOWNESS
15 · aite · Coniston · 16 · Bowmanstead · Sawrey · Storrs
Hall Dunnerdale · 529 · 22 · Brantwood · Hill Top · Hotel · Winste
Caw · 24 · Grizedale · Ferry
11 · Hoses · GRIZEDALE FOREST · 263
375 · 8 · Satterthwaite · 333 · A592
4 · Broughton Mills · 7 · Furness Fells · Thwaite Head · Bowland Bridge · A507
A593 · Lower Hawthwaite · 13 · e Forge · Stott Park Bobbin Mill · Cartmel Fell · Row
Woodland · Water Yeat · Rusland · Finsthwaite · The How · 215
Broughton in Furness · Blawith · Oxen Park · Lakeside · 321
Lowick · Colton · Bouth · Newby Bridge · Staveley-in-Cartmel
Ilthwaites · Foxfield · Grizebeck · 9 · A5092 · Spark Bridge · A590 · Backbarrow · Ayside · Witherslack · Mill Si
Green · Green Road Station · Gawthwaite · 5 · High Newton · Town End · A5
Kirkby-in-Furness · Broughton Beck · Penny Bridge · Haverthwaite · Field Broughton · Lindale · Meathop
Beck Side · Low Wood · Greenodd · 205 · 222
Soutergate · Shooting House Hill · 332 · FURNESS · Arrad Foot · Holme Island
A595 · 311 · Mansriggs · Canal Foot · Holker Hall · 5 · Cartmel · i
15 · ULVERSTON · Pennington · Holker · Allithwaite · GRANGE-OVER-SANDS
kam in · Ireleth · Swarthmoor · Swarthmoor Hall · Flookburgh · Cark · Kents Bank · Silverda
urness · Marton · Lindal in Furness · A590 · Great Urswick · Cartmel Sands · Ravenstown
DALTON-IN-

At-a-glance...

Walk	Page	Start	Nat. Grid Reference	Distance	Time	Height Gain
Black Combe	78	Whicham	SD 135826	8½ miles (13.5km)	4½ hrs	2,185ft (666m)
Blawith Common and Beacon Tarn	26	Brown Howe	SD 291911	3¾ miles (6km)	2 hrs	720ft (220m)
Cartmel and Hampsfield Fell	20	Cartmel	SD 377787	4 miles (6.5km)	2 hrs	705ft (215m)
Caw	48	Seathwaite	SD 229962	5¼ miles (8.2km)	3 hrs	1,755ft (535m)
Coniston Old Man	50	Coniston	SD 304975	5 miles (8km)	3 hrs	2,430ft (740m)
Dalegarth and Eskdale	12	Dalegarth	NY 172003	3 miles (5km)	1½ hrs	280ft (85m)
Dent and Kinniside Stone Circle	52	Cleator Moor	NY 030144	7 miles (11km)	3½ hrs	1,575ft (480m)
Devoke Water	14	Birker Fell	SD 171977	3 miles (5km)	1½ hrs	490ft (150m)
Dow Crag and Goat's Water	75	Torver	SD 285 945	7 miles (11.5km)	4 hrs	2,395ft (730m)
Dunnerdale Fells	37	Ulpha	SD 199920	5 miles (8km)	2½ hrs	1,395ft (425m)
Ennerdale	81	Ennerdale Bridge	NY 085154	11½ miles (18.5km)	5 hrs	835ft (255m)
Eskdale Moor and Burnmoor Tarn	40	Dalegarth, Eskdale	NY 173007	5¼ miles (8.5km)	2½ hrs	935ft (285m)
Four Passes	88	Wasdale Head	NY 187085	15 miles (24km)	8 hrs	4,430ft (1,350m)
Greendale Tarn, Seatallan and Middle Fell	46	Greendale	NY 144056	5 miles (8km)	3 hrs	2,460ft (750m)
Muncaster Fell	16	Muncaster	SD 097967	3 miles (5km)	1½ hrs	555ft (170m)
Pillar and Red Pike	85	Wasdale	NY 168068	10 miles (16km)	6 hrs	4,235ft (1,290m)
Ravenglass and Muncaster	23	Ravenglass	SD 085964	4½ miles (7km)	2 hrs	670ft (210m)
Scafell Pike and Scafell	72	Wasdale	NY 183075	5½ miles (9km)	4 hrs	3,610ft (1,100m)
Seathwaite Tarn	34	Seathwaite	SD 229962	4¾ miles (7.6km)	2½ hrs	1,065ft (325m)
St Bees Head	61	St Bees	NX 961117	8 miles (13km)	4 hrs	1,215ft (370m)
Tarn Hows Wood and Yewdale	31	Coniston	SD 304975	5½ miles (9km)	2½ hrs	885ft (270m)
Top o'Selside and Arnsbarrow Hill	43	High Nibthwaite	SD 296 909	6 miles (9.5km)	3 hrs	1,245ft (380m)
Torver Low Common	28	Torver	SD 288927	5¼ miles (8.5km)	2½ hrs	805ft (245m)
Torver Commons and Walna Scar	69	Coniston	SD 304975	8¼ miles (13.2km)	4 hrs	1,425ft (435m)
Ulpha Park	18	Duddon	SD 184902	4½ miles (7km)	2 hrs	720ft (220m)
Upper Eskdale and Great Moss	65	Brotherilkeld	NY 213011	8 miles (12.5km)	4 hrs	1,345ft (410m)
Wast Water	55	Wasdale	NY 151054	8 miles (12.5km)	3½ hrs	740ft (225m)
Wetherlam	58	High Tilberthwaite	NY 306010	5½ miles (8.8km)	3½ hrs	2,295ft (700m)

Comments

A wide and glorious exploration of the great swelling mound north of Millom that is Black Combe. The walk can be shortened by returning directly from the summit.

Wild and woolly, this circuit onto Blawith Common is typical of the rock-punctuated terrain that hallmarks all the Torver Commons.

A splendid walk from a delightful village to an ancient and curious fell-top structure. Great views, and you can explore the flora and fauna of limestone pavement, a rare opportunity in Lakeland.

Caw is an isolated summit, seemingly much bigger than it is, but having a spectacular panorama to offer those who reach its summit. High above the Duddon Valley, the fell has views in all directions.

An up-and-down ascent of one of Lakeland's most popular fells, first ascended by a tourist in 1792. Quarry spoil mars much of the ascent, but the summit rewards with spectacular views.

Riparian exploration leads to an ancient hall and church set amid broad-leaved woodland; a perfect place for picnics and messing about at the water's edge.

A taste of the Coast-to-Coast walk, tackling its first (or last) summit, and then skittering down into a delectable hidden valley and visiting a reconstructed stone circle.

Splendidly wild and untamed country amid lazy mountains and idling becks; extend or reduce the walk as you wish, but nothing will better a remote day around Devoke Water.

An interesting and beautiful approach to an ancient cross-valley thoroughfare, followed by a splendid romp along a ridge before descending to a lovely tarn at the foot of the cliffs of Dow Crag.

A wild and rugged exploration of rarely visited fells above the delectable Duddon Valley, a place where wolves once roamed.

A walk on the wild side into the traffic-free recesses of Ennerdale, and passing below the gaze of Pillar, Steeple and Great Gable. The walk can be shortened at a halfway point.

Discover a sense of place on this remote moor, walked by ancient man, crossed by corpses and wild horses. A lonely tarn beneath the highest of Lakeland fells is a splendid place to contemplate...anything.

A tour de force involving four Lakeland valleys, and the passes that link them; yet in spite of the evident distance and height gain, the walking is relatively straightforward.

In spite of a fair amount of ascent, this visit to Greendale and adjacent fells is well worth the effort, a peaceful retreat, with fine views and a splendid tarn beside which to relax.

A brief, simple and charming out-and-back ascent to a stunning viewpoint, one that embraces the very heart of Lakeland.

A long and demanding circuit of Mosedale at the head of Wasdale; wait for a long summer's day, when it will prove a most agreeable feast with some of the finest ingredients of Lakeland fell walking.

Follow in the footsteps of Romans, and visit the ancestral home of an ancient family before striking across country to visit a remote corn mill.

A massive undertaking, climbing to the two highest summits of England, and coming face-to-face with one of Lakeland's cliff-related challenges, Lord's Rake. Ideal for a fine summer's day.

One of the finest lakeside settings anywhere, high above the Duddon Valley and surrounded by outlying fells of the Coniston range. A return through streamside woodland brings you back to Dunnerdale.

A breezy romp above the cliffs north of St Bees, following in the steps of the Northern Coast-to-Coast walk before taking its leave and pursuing a gentle and pleasing return to the ancient settlement.

A fine ascent through Tarn Hows woodland to the lake itself, concludes with a scamper down beside Tom Gill to gain the woodlands of Yewdale; water in abundance and numerous fine waterfalls.

Offering a perfect opportunity to explore once lawless lands, the walk visits the highest point of ground between the southern aspects of Windermere and Coniston Water.

Venturing into an area of Lakeland that few will know about, this circuit will test your navigational mettle, but reward you with peace and quiet with only curlew and skylark for company.

A fine contrasting walk that begins along the shoreline of Coniston Water before climbing onto Torver Commons and the ancient packhorse route of Walna Scar.

Peace and tranquility in a place that once resounded to packhorse trains, drunken rowdiness and the cries of the lords of Millom as they hunted their domain.

A chance to explore one of the large and wild theatres of the Lakes, lurking beneath the highest of its summits, and surrounded by high fells.

An exhilarating crossing of the most famous screes in Britain, which fall into its deepest lake. The complexities of the scree traverse are contrasted by the ease of the opposite side of the lake.

Wetherlam is a relatively neglected summit even though it has a grandstand view of the Old Man of Coniston and Swirl How, and its ascent begins in one of the least well-known dales in Lakeland.

Introduction to the Lake District

It is hard to imagine there might be anyone left in Britain who is unfamiliar with the renowned beauties of Lakeland, yet each year the author meets people visiting the region for the first time. While tramping contentedly across Esk Hause late one idyllic afternoon many years ago, under the guise of working, he met a pack-toting couple convinced, or certainly hoping, that the shapely peak of Ill Crag was their intended objective, Scafell Pike. Regrettably, he disillusioned them, but they had read, somewhere, that amid Scafell's rocks there is, near the summit of the Pike, a small oasis of green grass, and on it they planned to pitch their tent in order to watch the sun rise. Their intention could not be faulted, but their act of faith was beyond comprehension; there is indeed a patch of grass that will take a tent, but not much more, but to travel from Kent, as they had, in search of it, merely served as a reminder of how charismatic the Lake District can be, and how taken for granted, by we frequent visitors, who should know better. After all, the author can still remember a school geography lesson almost 50 years ago when the master put up a colour slide of Napes Needle, and asked if anyone knew where or what it was. All but one in the class seemed to know the answer, but another ten years would pass before the one exception did, but in those soft grey dusky days of the author's youth, engrossed in the hardships and limitations of a coal mining community in Lancashire, he had never heard of the Lake District, let alone Napes Needle. There may well be many similarly disadvantaged folk out there, awaiting the discovery of Lakeland and all its wonders.

In 1634, three military gentlemen, a Captain, a Lieutenant and an 'Ancient', pursuing a 'Short Survey' of England, arrived at a place they described as 'like a solitary wilderness' with 'nothing but hideous, hanging Hills, and great Pooles, that, what in respect of the murmuring noyse of those great waters, and those high mountainous, tumbling, rocky Hills, a man would thinke he were in another world.'

It takes a moment to recognise the Lake District, even though the writer identifies the key features of the landscape clearly enough. What is disconcerting, like so much of the writing of the period, is the dominant sense of abhorrence, the use of the word 'hideous', which hints that although they are men of military character they nevertheless bear a sensitivity that quakes when faced with scenes that no modern writer would describe as hideous.

This dread of mountains persisted for some time. Yet things were soon to change. John Taylor, the so-called 'Water Poet' (who journeyed on foot from London to Edinburgh and beyond, and described the experience in *Penniless Pilgrimage*), felt the pull of the mountains. And did so at a time when the

Beside Coniston Water, Torver Commons

norm was still to look on mountainous areas with a fearful eye, as did Daniel Defoe, who described Westmoreland (sic) as being 'a country eminent only for being the wildest, most barren and frightful of any that I have passed over in England, or even in Wales it self; the west side, which borders on Cumberland, is indeed bounded by a chain of almost unpassable mountains, which, in the language of the country, are called Fells.'

In spite of these claims, people seem to have been climbing Skiddaw, at least, for some centuries. Bishop Nicolson of Carlisle, for example, went up with friends as early as 1684 ... for the mere pleasure of going there, which Ruskin's secretary, W. G. Collingwood notes '... seems to have been a well-known point of view.'

But quite when the modern cult of walking took off is not certain. The Victorians, keen on exploration and appreciation of the landscape, certainly came to the Lakes in large numbers, especially after the arrival of the railways in the mid-19th century. Captain Joseph Budworth rambled through the Lakes in 1792 and 1795, covering more than 240 miles. Unaffected by the prevailing Romantic mood, he walked freely among the fells and 'trundled boulders down Helvellyn', doing so for the experience and to enjoy himself. What is remarkable about his accounts of walking in the Lake District is the appealing frankness, which caused him to confess his own inadequacy as when he bandaged up one eye before crossing the fell slopes below Langdale Pikes, in order not to see what lay below. Budworth's ascent of the Old Man of Coniston is often cited as the first 'tourist' ascent of the mountain. That was barely 200 years ago, and as we romp the fells today it is difficult to imagine what it might have felt like to make the first, or, at least, the first recorded, exploration of the fells.

Wordsworth and the so-called Lake Poets are generally credited (or blamed, depending on your point of view), with bringing increasing numbers of tourists to the Lake District. That is neither entirely true nor fair, other writers were here before them. But Wordsworth lived in the Lake District and knew it intimately, and certain it is that his descriptive writings did much to attract visitors. Even so, the vogue for personal narratives masquerading as guidebooks went on well into the 19th century, most written on the basis of brief tours by outsiders. They were significant in creating a literary illusion, leaving little to the individual's imagination, directing their appreciation of the landscape rather than influencing or persuading independent exploration and discovery.

The Lake District today is all things to all men (and women). Each visitor sees the Lakeland landscape in a different way. Some describe the fells, others the dales, the rivers, lakes, tarns and meres. There are many landscape features, but overall, in a physical sense, it is the fells and the lakes that are the key to the region's popularity. And although water appears throughout the length and breadth of Britain, in the Lake District it is the presence of so much water in such a compact area set among dramatic fells and beautiful dales, themselves bounded north, west and south by even greater expanses of water, that makes this region so remarkably different from other parts of Britain, and so palpably unique – the 'Odd Corner of England' as it has been called.

Nor can it be overlooked that the Lake District comprises the only significant mountainous region in England, uniquely distinctive, so much so that the National Park Authority was able to adopt as its emblem the arrangement of fells at the head of Wasdale, arguably the most inaccessible dale for the vast majority of visitors. Yet it is a landscape arrangement at once symbolic, iconic and instantly recognisable.

The West and South-western Fells

The dales of western Lakeland are breathtakingly beautiful, rich in flora and fauna, wild moors, craggy heights, hidden dales and sundry secret ways, but they suffer from relative inaccessibility; there is no passage, other than on foot, through the middle of the Lakes to get into Wasdale, or Ennerdale (where, in any case, traffic is forbidden), although one early map of the region does rather ambitiously show a motor road crossing to Sty Head and down into Wasdale. Yet, for the walker, Ennerdale, Wasdale and Eskdale are as delectable as anywhere else, and arguably more so. It was in Wasdale that the early pioneers of Lakeland rock climbing came to cut their teeth, and, in a few sad instances, to die.

By comparison, the Coniston Fells, being much more accessible, are as popular as any in the Lake District. Between the two, one of Lakeland's hidden gems is to be found, Dunnerdale, the valley of the River Duddon. The river rises on Cold Pike and Pike o'Blisco above Langdale, but by the time it passes Cockley Beck in Wrynose Bottom, and changes direction to head for the sea, it has started to fashion the most breathtaking of dales, flanked by comparatively low fells, but summits that have great appeal and unrivalled views. This and the mosses north west of Coniston Water is the home of early man, who lived on the high moors of Torver, Blawith and Monk Coniston. For these early settlers their main interest lay in the extensive woodlands, a great DIY storehouse from which to build their homes, construct weapons and tools.

In the early 12th century, much of the area, known as Furness, was given to a colony of monks from the Norman-French abbey at Savigny. They founded an abbey at Furness, and in 1143 resisted the parent abbey's move to the Cistercian Order, for which the abbot, Peter of York, was captured and held in France, becoming a most worthy monk and learning the Cistercian Order. It was the influence of the abbey that shaped much of the landscape we see today around Coniston, for it was the monks, rather than settling Scandinavians, who cleared most of the forest to make charcoal to fire the bloomeries for the copper mines and to develop grazing for sheep.

Only with the opening of the Furness Railway in 1859, originally intended for more efficient transportation of copper and slate, did tourism begin. By the time author and art critic John Ruskin came to the live on the shores of Coniston Water, tourism was well established; Keswick and Ambleside had a host of new and old hotels, while a complete new town had developed at Windermere, a town of hotels, lodging-houses, inns and shops.

The west and the south have a distinct feeling of *entrée*. This is the way people used to access the region. In the days before motorways, trunk roads and, for that matter, anything resembling a passable highway, visitors would reach the area across the treacherous sands of Morecambe Bay, arriving at Grange and Cartmel, where the bodies of many who failed to beat the incoming tide lie buried, including, from 1577 'One little mann Rownd faced wch was Drouned at Grainge'. Out on the coast, Whitehaven has a long legacy as a seaport from which coal was conveyed from the West Cumbrian mines mainly of the Lowther family; while nearby St Bees is the traditional landing site of St Bega, who came from Ireland and developed a priory here.

When the heart of Lakeland is beating to the rhythm of 10,000 feet, the pace of life in the west and south is much more relaxed, and the moors and mosses repose in stark but complimentary contrast to the highest fells in England.

This book includes a list of waypoints alongside the description of the walk, so that you can enjoy the full benefits of gps should you wish to. For more information on using your gps, read the *Pathfinder® Guide GPS for Walkers*, by gps teacher and navigation trainer, Clive Thomas (ISBN 978-0-7117-4445-5). For essential information on map reading and basic navigation, read the *Pathfinder® Guide Map Reading Skills* by outdoor writer, Terry Marsh (ISBN 978-0-7117-4978-8). Both titles are available in bookshops or can be ordered online at www.totalwalking.co.uk

Dalegarth and Eskdale

		GPS waypoints
Start	Dalegarth	
Distance	3 miles (5km)	NY 172 003
Height gain	280 feet (85m)	Ⓐ NY 172 001
Approximate time	1½ hours	Ⓑ NY 188 004
Parking	Trough House Bridge	Ⓒ NY 189 007
Route terrain	Woodland; riverside paths	
Ordnance Survey maps	Landranger 89 (West Cumbria), Explorer OL6 (The English Lakes – South-western area)	

An absolute gem of a walk; simple, delightful, easy and surrounded by extravagant beauty. This rewarding circuit should take less than two hours, but could just so easily waylay you for much more than that. Link it in with a ride on the miniature railway from Ravenglass, and you can enjoy a full day amid the most superb scenery

From the parking area at Trough House Bridge, where the Esk skitters through a scenic mélange of trees, rocks and bubbling streams, turn left to follow a surfaced lane to a bend opposite Dalegarth Hall.

Dalegarth Hall was built in 1599 (some say it dates from the 14th century), and boasts magnificent chimneys; it is the ancient manor house of Austhwaite, and home to the Stanley family.

Continue a short way farther to a track junction Ⓐ, and here turn left through a gate and follow a descending track across an enclosed pasture.

(Anyone wanting to visit Stanley Ghyll Force, a popular destination for adventurous Victorian travellers, should remain on the original track to view this dramatic fall in a deep and narrow gorge, and then return to the same point.)

Beyond the pasture, bear right to a footbridge spanning a tributary of the Esk, which is close by. On passing through another gate, keep right for a few strides, and then take a broad track that swings left across rough ground, with St Catherine's Church putting in an appearance through the trees on your left.

When you arrive at a wall gap, go to the right and walk around a wall corner. The track wanders on through a delightful thin belt of woodland much favoured by great spotted woodpeckers. Keep on to pass a small tarn, surrounded by larch, and with a convenient bench on which to rest and reflect for a while.

Another footbridge spans a busy beck, after which the track runs on to Low Birker Farm, with lovely views to the left of Scafell, Slight Side and the nearer shapely profiles of Great and Little Barrow. On reaching Low Birker Ⓑ, descend left to pass the buildings, and then walk along the access track to arrive at the single span of Doctor Bridge Ⓒ.

Cross the bridge and turn left on the other side, through a gate and along a path for St Catherine's Church. You

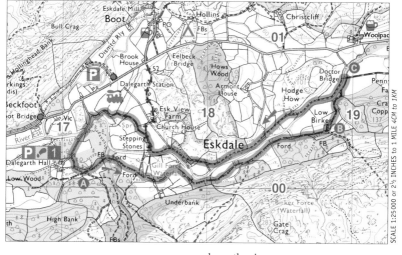

0	200	400	600	800 METRES	1
					KILOMETRES
					MILES
0	200	400	600 YARDS	½	

soon reach a riverside bench, which would be a perfect place for a picnic.

The return path is every bit as delightful and straightforward as the outward leg, with the added attraction that it passes a fascinating display of dry-stone walls. After a short stretch between such walls, the path breaks out into a rough grassy pasture dotted with gorse and bracken, and later becomes a fine terraced path across a steep bank

Eskdale landscape

above the river.

The path does eventually come down to run alongside the river, as it approaches St Catherine's Church. Cradled by the Esk, St Catherine's Church dates from the 12th century, when the Priory at St Bees owned a chapel here. It is an enchanting setting, and the graveyard host to the local yeomen of Eskdale times past.

Take the walled track to the right of the church, but after about 100 yds, turn left onto an enclosed path, which eventually emerges to meet a surfaced lane. Turn left to return to Trough House Bridge, and complete the walk. ●

Devoke Water

		GPS waypoints
Start	Birker Fell	
Distance	3 miles (5km)	SD 171 977
Height gain	490 feet (150m)	Ⓐ SD 162 970
Approximate time	1½ hours	Ⓑ SD 152 969
Parking	Roadside parking spaces	
Route terrain	Rugged mountain tops and tracks; *not advised in poor visibility*	
Ordnance Survey maps	Landranger 96 (Barrow-in-Furness & South Lakeland), Explorer OL6 (The English Lakes – South-western area)	

There seems more to this simple walk than there is. The illusion is created by the vastness of the moorland bowl in which Devoke Water reposes, one where the adjacent fells stand back and so give a distorted sense of their height. But the beauty is in the solitude and away-from-it-all-ness, a quality that is a perfect antidote to the bustle of everyday life. Throw in the fact that so few visitors to Lakeland take the trouble to find this lovely tarn, and connoisseurs of peace and quiet will find it in abundance here.

The key to the start is a minor road junction on the Birker Fell road, where a rusting roadside signpost marks the departure of a bridleway, a broad track, racing off in a westerly direction. The track soon passes a gate and then

Linbeck Gill and Water Crag

brings Devoke Water into view, on its shores a partially ruined boat house Ⓐ to which the track leads.

(This may be a sufficient walk for some, and the shores of the tarn, close by the boat house, a perfect place to take it all in and then retreat. Strong walkers may want to head for the hills that lie to the south of the tarn. The appearance of considerable height and ruggedness is deceptive, but to bring Yoadcastle and White Pike into the equation will add both immeasurably and pleasurably to the day. There is no evident path to start the ascent, but none is needed, and the joy of navigating through low crags and across the tops is paramount.)

Devoke Water is the largest tarn in the Lake District, almost a mile in length, and one of the highest at 775 feet (236m). There is an outflow from the tarn at its north-western corner, where Linbeck Gill flows gently for a short distance before plunging down gushing miniature waterfalls and through a stunning, narrow gorge.

From the boat house, the ongoing track round the tarn is generally clear but intermittently boggy. Your objective is a cairn  **B** on the western skyline beyond the end of the lake. It is difficult to imagine it now, but the whole of this area was covered by trees 3,000 years ago. Indeed, the western end of this upland hideaway was peopled in Bronze Age times, as more than 400 hut circles, cairns, enclosures and ancient field systems testify. Tempting though it is to lay at the door of the Scandinavian settlers the blame for the deforestation of the Lake District, that would not be entirely fair. Certainly, the Vikings cleared large tracts of forest, but the rot started when Bronze Age Man stopped living as a nomadic hunter-gatherer and became a settled farmer in need of space in which to plant crops.

A clear path leads up to the cairn, on which there is a low windbreak shelter. From here, the route crosses Linbeck Gill, and generally this is not a problem, although it is easier to cross nearer the

outflow from the tarn than it is farther west once the water has started on its turbulent dash through the Linbeck gorge. If the beck is in spate, it may be wiser to backtrack than to attempt a potentially hazardous leap of faith.

Once beyond the beck, a clear grassy path climbs on to Water Crag, which proves a lovely vantage point, and a good place to seek out a cranny in which to take a break. The top is surmounted by a large cairn, but there is higher ground, an outcrop of red granite, a little to the north.

From Water Crag, a continuing grassy path leads across to Rough Crag, another fine fell with a view out across the windswept grasslands of Birker Fell, and far to the north east and the heart of Lakeland, where the Scafells rule the roost.

One more minor top awaits: Pike How almost overlooks the starting point on the Birker Fell road, and its conquest, a simple grassy plod, will faze no one. From there it is literally downhill all the way across tussocky terrain to rejoin the road.

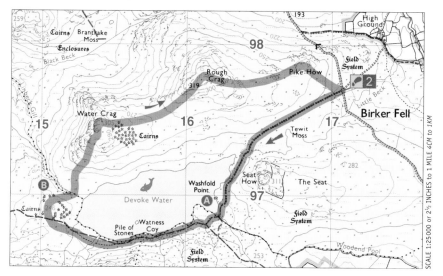

Muncaster Fell

		GPS waypoints
Start	Muncaster	
Distance	3 miles (5km)	🖉 SD 097 967
Height gain	555 feet (170m)	Ⓐ SD 106 976
Approximate time	1½ hours	Ⓑ SD 110 981
Parking	Car park opposite entrance to Muncaster Castle	
Route terrain	Rugged fell tops and rough tracks	
Ordnance Survey maps	Landranger 96 (Barrow-in-Furness & South Lakeland), Explorer OL6 (The English Lakes – South-western area)	

Anyone drawn to thinking that to get a good view or a great walk you have to head for the heights, will be delighted and probably amazed by Muncaster Fell. It ranks as a Marilyn (for those who like to tick lists), but has no significant elevation. Yet relative to the surrounding countryside it is huge, sandwiched between the valleys of the Mite and the Esk.

This walk keeps things simple, and opts for a brief burst up to the summit and back, although it is possible to devise a much longer walk by continuing along the knobbly ridge to Muncaster Head and then returning at a lower level. But this involves a fair bit of time in the gloom of a conifer plantation, when the real attractions of openness, wide-ranging views and craggy summits lie above.

🖉 Begin from the car park opposite the entrance to Muncaster Castle, and turn left along the road. *For safety's sake, you need to cross the road to the footpath opposite and then recross it a little farther on when the footpath changes sides.* Continue only as far as the point where the A595 bends to the right. (For a much safer option, begin along a bridleway from a gate at the rear of the car park, and follow a broad track across a field. When the track meets a farm access at a T-junction, turn right and walk out to meet the A595 at the bend.)

Now walk into Fell Lane, a clear and almost straight bridleway that rises steadily. The straight nature of Fell Lane is a clue to its origins, for this was a Roman road linking their fort at Ravenglass (Glannaventa) with Hardknott (Mediobogdum). Apart

Summit of Muncaster Fell

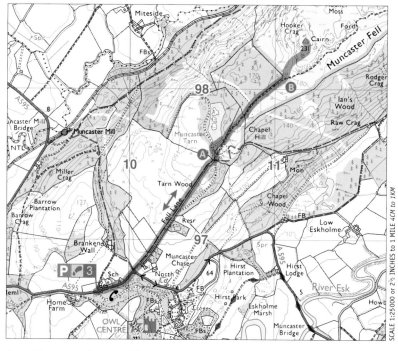

from this stretch, the rest of the Roman route across the fell has been lost, although a little farther to the north-east is what appears to be a Stone Age dolmen, identified as Ross's Camp, which may well be of Roman derivation.

Eventually the track does descend as it approaches a junction **A**. Here, turn left to discover Muncaster Tarn, and turn right at the tarn edge on a broad track, which continues around the tarn. But after only 100 yds, branch right to rejoin the original route.

As you reach a gate the ascent eases and Muncaster Fell now comes into view. The path now takes a delightful course across open fell moorland. Two paths materialise just beyond overhead powerlines; one cuts a green swathe through bracken, the other bears left to follow a fenceline around the edge of a large area of cleared woodland.

At a fence corner **B** the path again divides. To the left you gain a low ridge and then a clear path climbing directly

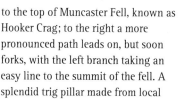

to the top of Muncaster Fell, known as Hooker Crag; to the right a more pronounced path leads on, but soon forks, with the left branch taking an easy line to the summit of the fell. A splendid trig pillar made from local stone and perched on a rocky plinth is a reminder of the skill that went into covering the whole country with these now obsolete pillars.

Just below the summit are numerous nooks and crannies, making this a perfect place to visit with children and enjoy a picnic. To the south rises the great dome of Black Combe (see Walk 25), and to the south-east the massive moorland sprawl of Ulpha Fell. It is to the north-east, however, that your gaze will alight on the high central fells of Lakeland, radiating from the Scafell Pikes.

The return journey simply retraces the outward route. ●

Ulpha Park

		GPS waypoints
Start	Duddon	🖊 SD 184 902
Distance	4½ miles (7km)	Ⓐ SD 188 916
Height gain	720 feet (220m)	Ⓑ SD 189 925
Approximate time	2 hours	Ⓒ SD 194 899
Parking	Limited roadside parking at Logan Beck Bridge	
Route terrain	Rough tracks; farmland; woodland; some road walking	
Ordnance Survey maps	Landranger 96 (Barrow-in-Furness & South Lakeland), Explorer OL6 (The English Lakes – South-western area)	

On the edge of untamed moorland, this circuit of Ulpha Park is quite uncomplicated and especially delightful in early spring when the woodlands are bright with daffodils; later the woods are heady with the scent of wild garlic. The seeming simplicity and tranquility of the area belies a sometimes, turbulent past.

🖊 Cross the bridge and take the second turning on the right, a walled lane beyond a gate, rising as a stony track along the flanks of craggy Penn. With fell on one side and woodland on the other, the route is remarkably peaceful and quiet, with the chance of spotting the occasional deer slipping silently through the serried ranks of spruce.

Eventually, the track arrives at a gate, where it leaves the woodland for a more open aspect. A short way farther on Ⓐ, with fine views to the right of the Dunnerdale Fells among which Stickle Pike and Caw are especially prominent, you can bear right along a permissive path to visit the ivy-clad ruins of Frith Hall. Frith Hall, sometime hunting lodge, overlooks the deer park hunted by the men of the Huddleston family from Millom Castle. Later, the hall became a rudimentary inn open to all, a boisterous stop-over for packhorse trains, and like many routes that are

linked to the coast the area also attracted smugglers not least from the Isle of Man, an island once described as a 'warehouse of frauds'. As a result, strong alcohol was always readily available at Frith Hall, making it considerably more lively and rowdy a place than it is today. It is even rumoured that the hall was used as a venue for weddings, à la Gretna Green, and that at least one murder was committed here.

In time, the hall became the nucleus of a farm, and it still stands amid farmland where the ubiquitous Herdwick sheep crop the turf in silence. If places can be described as evocative, carrying in their atmosphere traces of the past, then this is one such. The setting is superb, commanding a splendid position above the Duddon Valley.

Beyond Frith Hall the old highway drops to a gate at single-arched Bleabeck Bridge. Continue beyond on a gently rising track for Mill Brow, with

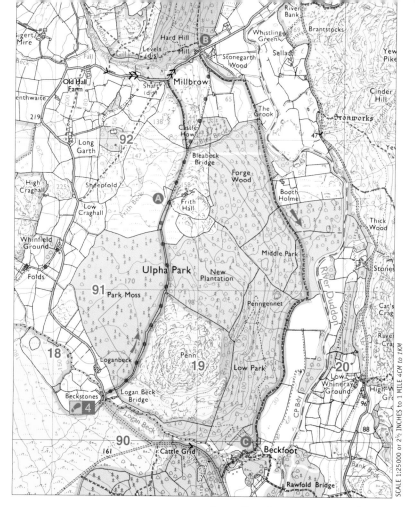

SCALE 1:25000 or 2½ INCHES to 1 MILE 4CM to 1KM

the fulsome breast of Castle How immediately ahead, set against the even more buxom mound of The Pike. The track comes out to meet a narrow lane, descending steeply, with a fine view of Caw, and, among the Coniston Fells, White Maiden, Swirl How and Grey Friar.

At the foot of Mill Brow stands a tall, ivy-rich chimney and two cottages. This is the site of Ulpha Mill, dating from the 18th century, when it provided wooden bobbins for the Lancashire cotton trade.

When you reach the tall chimney **B**, leave the road by turning right onto a broad footpath for Beckfoot. Shortly, when the track forks, bear left, descending. At a gate you enter the woodlands of Ulpha Park, everywhere strewn with daffodils in springtime. This is a splendid interlude, and of sufficient length and quality to give botanists plenty of cause for delay. But eventually, you arrive at Beckfoot **C**, a cluster of houses and farm buildings, through which the route keeps forward to cross Beckfoot Bridge. Beyond, you follow a surfaced lane out to join the Corney Fell road.

Turn right, and climb steadily above wood-ravined Logan Beck. Just as you finally escape the trees and break out onto the open moorland of Thwaites Fell, branch right onto a side road for Ulpha, and soon complete the walk at Logan Beck Bridge. ●

Cartmel and Hampsfield Fell

		GPS waypoints	
Start	Cartmel	🖉 SD 377 787	
Distance	4 miles (6.5km)	Ⓐ SD 396 788	
Height gain	705 feet (215m)	Ⓑ SD 393 781	
Approximate time	2 hours	Ⓒ SD 388 784	
Parking	Cartmel, near race course		
Route terrain	Farmland; limestone upland; golf course		
Ordnance Survey maps	Landranger 96 (Barrow-in-Furness & South Lakeland), Explorer OL7 (The English Lakes – South-eastern area)		

Cartmel is one of those places that everyone instantly takes to: an agreeable mish-mash of history and antiquity from its 12th-century priory to its market cross and adjacent fish slabs that are a reminder of how dependent this settlement was on produce from the nearby Morecambe Bay. The curious structure on Hampsfield Fell, by contrast, was built in 1830, a 'hospice' for the use of visitors and others...an odd turn of phrase, for what exactly might 'others' be if not visitors?

In 2008, Cartmel Racecourse won a significant award when it was named Small Racecourse of the Year; not bad for a course that has fixtures on barely a handful of days in the year.

🖉 From the car park, walk into the village centre to encounter the market cross and fish slabs standing in front of the priory gatehouse, probably built between 1330 and 1340. When the priory was surrendered to Henry VIII's men in 1536, the gatehouse was one of only a few places to be spared, probably because it was used as a courthouse.

Keep forward towards the priory buildings, and enter the church grounds. The church is a huge and solid edifice founded by Augustinian canons between 1190 and 1220; much of the priory was destroyed during the Dissolution of the Monasteries, but the church remained, as at Bolton Abbey in Yorkshire's Wharfedale, because it was (and still is) the parish church.

The Dissolution destroyed much more than buildings, it also destroyed the priory's financial record, the chartulary, which among other things detailed the appointment of guides to Morecambe Bay whose obligation was to safeguard the crossing of the treacherous sands. Alas, such records as do exist only take us back to 1501, although it is certain that guides were appointed much earlier than this.

Follow the path around the church to emerge on a side road. Turn right and walk out to a road junction. Cross the road and turn left, but soon leave it by ascending a short flight of steps onto an enclosed path (Cistercian Way) that gives into a large open pasture. Keep to the right-hand edge of the pasture and cross to a gate giving onto an access track at Pit Farm. Turn left along the access but almost immediately leave it by branching right past farm buildings to enter another field.

Cross the field diagonally to a gate at the left-hand edge of a hedgerow from which there is a fine retrospective view to Cartmel. Through the gate take a track swinging left to run alongside a wall; you soon leave the track as it passes through a gate. Now simply climb beside the wall, and at a metal kissing-gate you pass through the intake wall, and begin the final pull onto Hampsfield Fell.

The view northwards extends from Caw and the Coniston Fells, round to the Langdale Pikes, Helvellyn and the Fairfield Horseshoe. As the gradient eases you stroll a close-cropped sward of greenness and are plainly on limestone, which is a nice touch as from here you can see across to the limestone dales of Yorkshire, amid which flat-topped Ingleborough can easily be picked out.

At a track junction **A**, turn left and climb easily to a through-stile in a limestone wall, which marks the boundary of the Lake District National Park. Beyond, a simple romp takes you up to the hospice.

The top of Hamspfield Fell (also called Hampsfell) is divided by walls into enclosures that date from the passing of the *Parliamentary Enclosure Act* in the early 19th century. At a slight distance from the hospice, and worth exploring, are large tracts of limestone pavement, rich in lime-loving plants like maidenhair, spleenwort, hart's-tongue fern and other limestone ferns. These species are not instantly evident, because they grow in the fissures, known as grikes, between the limestone blocks – the horizontal planes of limestone being known as clints. What is perhaps more obvious are large boulders, which anyone can see are not of the same rock type. These are erratics, carried here by retreating

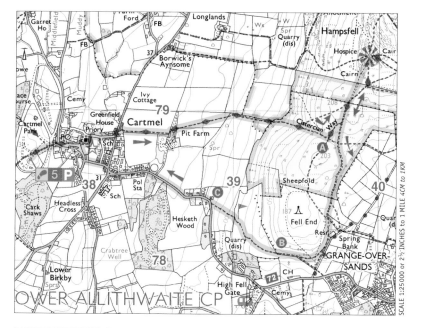

Hampsfell Hospice

building, but then passing to the right of it. Beyond, you come into an area of scattered boulders and hawthorn, to reach another waymark, where the path divides.

Keep to the right, following the more prominent path, which brings you into sight of a stile at the bottom left corner of a field and with a golf course directly in front of you **B**. There is no need to descend to the stile, when you can bear right from a slightly higher point, following a clear path that gradually closes in on the golf course.

Walk to a waymark, where the path passes through a spread of gorse. Then, as the path swings to the right, cross to a ladder-stile giving onto the golf course. The way across the course is waymarked, but is not always obvious. Begin by walking down a line of conifers, which takes you down to a raised tee. Pass this, and keep on in the same direction. The way is not clear, but you are targeting the fifth tee, behind which (unseen from above) there is a low ladder-stile at which you leave the golf course, to walk down a sloping field and reach a road **C**.

Now turn right and follow the lane down towards Cartmel. Turn left at the **Pig and Whistle pub**, and at the next junction turn right, but first take a quick look at an ancient roadside sign here indicating the distance to Lancaster via the Over-Sands Route. Walk into the village centre, and there turn left towards the market cross and forward to the racecourse to complete the walk. ●

glaciers and then dumped as the weight of the rock proved too much for the weakening ice flows. These limestone pavements are not only host to a wealth of plants, but are equally renowned as a superb habitat for butterflies, with 24 species so far recorded here.

Not surprisingly, the Hampsfell pavements are protected by a Limestone Pavement Order, under the provisions of the *Wildlife and Countryside Act, 1981*.

Many paths radiate from the top of the fell, but to continue, return to the wall and back down towards the path junction **A**, but before reaching the junction, bear left when the track divides. The track shortly swings across a hill slope, bringing the long peninsula of Humphrey Head into view. You come down to a gate in a wall, beyond which keep forward across a large sloping pasture. As you descend into a dip, which contains a pile of stones and small boulders, turn left to a waymark pole. At the waymark, branch right towards a small square reservoir

Ravenglass and Muncaster

Start	Ravenglass	
Distance	4½ miles (7km)	
Height gain	670 feet (210m)	
Approximate time	2 hours	
Parking	Free parking in Ravenglass	
Route terrain	Woodland; farmland; managed parkland	
Ordnance Survey maps	Landranger 96 (Barrow-in-Furness & South Lakeland), Explorer OL6 (The English Lakes – South-western area)	

GPS waypoints

- 🖉 SD 085 964
- Ⓐ SD 093 957
- Ⓑ SD 099 960
- Ⓒ SD 099 969
- Ⓓ SD 097 976
- Ⓔ SD 093 966

A view across a lovely estuary, where three rivers have their confluence, is Ravenglass's outlook on the world: a shingle beach, a few small yachts waiting companionably for the tide, and a steady trade in birdlife. This one-street village, the only coastal village within the Lake District National Park, was granted a market charter as long ago as the 13th century, and has a history to match. From it, this walk ventures inland to the privately owned Muncaster Castle, before taking an extra dip into local history by visiting the Muncaster Mill on the banks of the River Mite.

🖉 Set off from the car park, passing between buildings to turn left along the village street – there is only one to choose from – and at its end, bear left to locate a passageway beneath the railway line. Cross a narrow lane beyond, and then turn right on a footpath that leads directly to the Bath House that once served the Roman fort of Glannoventa.

There are substantial remains of the bath house, although without the nearby interpretation panel it is difficult to make much sense of the layout. The site of the fort, of which only earthen shapes remain, was largely on the opposite side of the narrow lane, and part was destroyed when the railway was constructed.

From the 1st to the 3rd century CE, more than 1,000 soldiers occupied the fort at Ravenglass, which served as a vital command and supply centre for the Roman occupation of the north-western part of England. Some authorities conjecture that Ravenglass was the southernmost of a string of Roman coastal defences around Cumbria, extending south from Hadrian's Wall; others suggest that the fort was not known as Glannoventa at all, but rather Itunocelum.

Keep on past the bath house, and when the roadside path ends, bear left onto a broad track that leads up to Newtown House. Ignore the first path for Muncaster branching on the left, and keep on until level with the buildings, when you can take either a gate on the left or walk a few strides farther to a signposted footpath Ⓐ. Both combine almost instantly, but then divide again. Take the right branch, following a path that plunges you into the murkiness of a dense conifer plantation. Mercifully, this is relatively short-lived, and before long you shake off the trees to clamber over a stile into a large pasture, a former deer park belonging to Muncaster Castle. Now continue in a north-easterly direction, keeping to the right of a low rocky knoll on the left, but without any discernible footpath to confirm the direction.

Maintain the same direction, and as you cross the pasture so a distant wall comes into view, and then a signpost, which pinpoints the location of a gate **B** giving into the grounds of Muncaster Castle. A delightful path then leads through bluebell woodland, and on beneath a wide range of exotic trees and shrubs. When the path forks, branch right to see a view of the castle that now appears below. The path gradually descends to intercept a broad track.

The path just travelled is a right of way through the grounds, and it continues now across a grassy area towards the Stables Yard ahead. Walk up a surfaced lane to the left of the Stables Yard and soon you will reach the church, and then walk out to meet the A595.

With the exception of the facility to use **toilets** *(opposite the plant centre gates, near the church) and the purchase of light refreshments from the* **Owl Garden Tea Shop***, it is important to realise that the ability to walk along the right of way does not carry with it the right to leave it and explore the castle grounds (for which you need a 'Walker's Ticket', available only to those arriving at Muncaster by public footpaths).*

Muncaster Castle *(see page 95 for details)* is the ancient seat of the Pennington family, a lineage that has survived for more than 800 years thanks, it is said, to the ongoing survival intact of a glass drinking bowl – known as the Luck of Muncaster – given to the family by Henry VI with the earnest prayer that the family might prosper so long as the bowl remained unbroken. The regal gesture was in response to hospitality given to the king after he was found wandering the fells following the Battle of Towton in 1461 during the Wars of the Roses (the largest and bloodiest ever fought on British soil), although authorities argue that it may have been after the Battle of Hexham three years later. The glass bowl has remained intact ever since, and its whereabouts are a closely guarded family secret.

On reaching the A595, cross it and turn left, walking to a nearby bend. Go forward, leaving the road, onto a farm access track that leads to Branken Wall Farm. Walk as far as a gate **C** on the right, opposite the end of a track arriving from the left. Turn right through the gate into woodland, and follow the ongoing track until it divides into three. Take either the middle or the

Remains of the Roman Bath House, Ravenglass

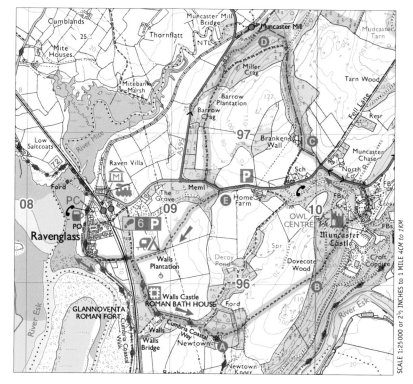

left track. The former takes you down to a broad track behind Muncaster Mill; the latter effects a shortcut.

Muncaster Mill (not open to the public) is a water-powered mill dating from 1455. The present building, however, dates from the early 18th century, and electricity was generated by the mill until 1958, using a waterwheel. It is possible that the Romans may have used the mill, or at least the site of it, as the Mite is tidal to this point. The mill was part of the Pennington Estate until 1970.

If you took the path down to the mill, then on reaching the broad track, you need to turn left, but to take the higher of two tracks, a path for Ravenglass, rising on the left **D**. This crosses poorly drained ground and is often muddy in places. The path rises to meet a path from the left, which is the alternative path used by those taking the shortcut mentioned above.

Now continue climbing gently to leave the woodland at a gate, after which the track continues ascending across a gorsey landscape above the estuary of the River Mite. Eventually, the route emerges on the A595. Cross the road and turn left, walking for about 100 yds, and then leaving the road for a footpath on the right **E**, leading into light woodland.

You leave the woodland at a kissing-gate, from which you strike across rough pasture in a south-westerly direction, following a grassy path to a gate in a mid-field fence. Through the gate, turn right alongside the fence and follow it out to meet the narrow lane and path used earlier in the walk. Now go forward across the lane and under the railway line to return to Ravenglass and complete the walk. ●

Blawith Common and Beacon Tarn

		GPS waypoints	
Start	Brown Howe, Coniston shore	🖉 SD 291 911	
Distance	3¾ miles (6km)	Ⓐ SD 286 901	
Height gain	720 feet (220m)	Ⓑ SD 281 899	
Approximate time	2 hours	Ⓒ SD 275 905	
Parking	At start		
Route terrain	Road walking; moorland fells; lake shore paths; minor unenclosed road to finish		
Ordnance Survey maps	Landranger 97 (Kendal & Morecambe), Explorer OL6 (The English Lakes – South-western area)		

Blawith Common is of the same ilk as the rest of the Torver Commons; low-lying hillocks that punctuate a landscape of brackeny bogland. It all makes for a fascinating experience amid an area not subject to mass invasion, but rather more to peaceful contemplation, a feature it shares admirably with Torver Low Common to the north west (see Walk 8). You can combine the two walks into something much longer, but you will need a day of good visibility. The key is to turn it into a figure-of-eight walk, starting at Brown Howe.

🖉 The walk starts from a car park on the shores of Coniston Water, which can prove a lovely disincentive to make a start for a while. But, leave the car park and turn left along the road, taking care against approaching traffic. Cross the road and go past a road junction *and, for safety (but not of necessity), shortly afterwards take to a rough track ascending, on the right, towards a disused quarry.*

Just before the quarry entrance, bear left onto a grassy path through bracken. This path, roughly parallel with the road below, involves dodging below branches, and shortly leads back down to the road.

Continue along the road, with great care, until, having passed two parking areas on the left (Blawith Common), a track is reached on the right Ⓐ, just as the road bends left. The track rises steadily onto brackeny slopes, the way forward never quite certain in terms of seeing where you are going. But there is a clear path underfoot.

Near overhead powerlines the track forks. Branch left Ⓑ, still climbing. Eventually the path crosses the shoulder of Slatestone Fell and descends to a path junction, close by a wooden footbridge. Turn right, and follow the path through a landscape of undulating bracken hummocks punctuated by low, rock outcrops. When the path next forks, close by stepping stones bridging a stream, turn right, crossing the stones and walking on to the edge of Beacon

Tarn, which remains concealed until the very last moment.

Speculation invariably arises among readers of Arthur Ransome's books about where is the place he called Swallowdale. Of course, the author never disclosed his locations, but at Beacon Tarn you may be forgiven for thinking you are very close.

Beacon Tarn is surprisingly large, almost a lake, and must be the 'Trout Tarn' of 'Swallowdale' *(Swallows and Amazons, 1930)*, in which Roger was taught how to 'guddle' trout. North east of the tarn rises Beacon Fell, a neat craggy summit with fascinating outcrops.

At the water's edge, turn left. Across the next section numerous paths diverge, typical of the area, but the immediate objective is simply to walk around the tarn, keeping to an obvious path that leads the way – this is, in fact,

part of the Cumbria Way, a popular Lakeland medium-distance walk. Beyond the northerly edge of the tarn, a grassy path ascends through a gap between low-lying fells 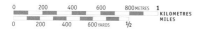, and provides outstanding views of the Coniston Fells ahead.

After the gap, the path descends steadily to pass a low-lying marshy area, which may well have contained another tarn not so many years ago, and slips easily through another shallow col before moving out onto a broad expanse of mossland.

Gradually the path starts heading for the distant green cone of Coats Hill and the minor road by which the walk concludes. When the descending path forks, branch left, staying on the more prominent of two paths.

Eventually, when the path meets the road, turn right, and follow it through an agreeable birch and ash landscape to meet the main road at a T-junction, only a short distance from the entrance to the Brown Howe car park. ●

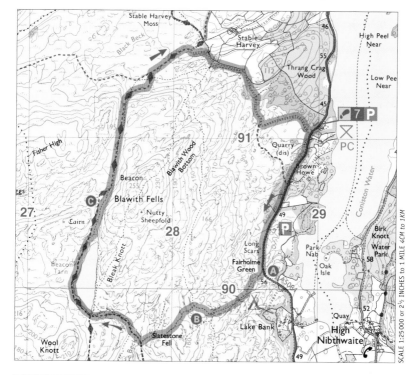

Torver Low Common

Start	Torver	**GPS waypoints**	
Distance	5¼ miles (8.5km)	🖉 SD 288 927	
Height gain	805 feet (245m)	Ⓐ SD 280 923	
		Ⓑ SD 276 930	
Approximate time	2½ hours	Ⓒ SD 264 923	
Parking	Roadside parking area at start	Ⓓ SD 268 916	
Route terrain	Rough moorland; *not advised in poor visibility*	Ⓔ SD 279 914	
Ordnance Survey maps	Landranger 97 (Kendal & Morecambe), Explorer OL6 (The English Lakes – South-western area)		

There is immense pleasure in finding somewhere peaceful when all around folk are heading for the hills. Torver Low Common is one such place, but it is a labyrinth of pathways across a skylark-loud mosaic of hummocks and hollows that will test the navigational mettle of anyone without it especially mattering whether you get it right or wrong.

🖉 The walk has an idyllic beginning, setting off by crossing the road and going through a kissing-gate onto a descending track that leads down to the busy waters of Torver Beck, about to enter Coniston Water from its journey in the gathering grounds of Goat's Water below Dow Crag. Cross a nearby footbridge, almost always preferable to the often-submerged stepping stones that saw duty in days of yore.

Once over the bridge, head steadily upwards into a long valley with steep sides that runs roughly in a south-westerly direction, and makes use of a lovely terraced path teasing a way through juniper and gorse. This early stage of the walk is part of the Cumbria Way.

Keep following the path up towards Torver Low Common, until you reach an obvious grassy Y-junction in the middle of bracken Ⓐ. Here, turn right, soon bringing Torver Tarn into view, and joining another path, then crossing a small stream. Within strides the path divides; take that on the right as it passes above the tarn. The path climbs across the flank of Anne Riggs, but once beyond the tarn, look for a path

Stepping stones, Torver Beck

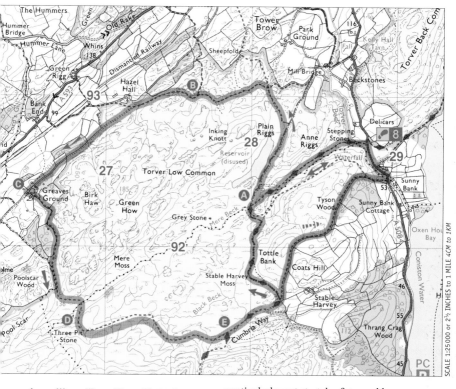

SCALE 1:25 000 or 2½ INCHES to 1 MILE 4CM to 1KM

branching left across a short stretch of boggy ground before continuing as a grassy path through bracken dotted with juniper bushes. Only a short way farther on, the path divides again in a way that is typical of this terrain.

There are numerous paths all setting off purposefully in one direction or another, and in some ways you can work out your own route linking the key points. But the route described here has the benefit of certainty, and is continuous; *even so, it should not be attempted in poor visibility.*

Once more branch left, passing beneath overhead powerlines. The next time the path divides, about 100 yds farther on, bear right, ignoring the track climbing up onto Plain Riggs. Just before a stream, the track divides again. Now, go left and within seconds, at a particularly wet stretch of ground bear left again. To be sure of your location, look to the right to see a wall gap about 100 yds away.

The path finds a lovely way around numerous small hillocks, with other paths thrown in to add to the confusion. But then a narrow lane comes into view off to your right. The path divides again, close by a small reedy tarn **B**. Here, keep to the left to pass around the westerly end of the tarn.

By maintaining a roughly westerly direction, the path does come down to intercept that narrow lane close by the turning into Hazel Hall Farm. Turn left along the lane, and follow this for about ³/₄ mile. This is a quiet lane with ample verges and leads through an area of Lakeland that few will know. Go past Rose Hill and through a gate to reach Greaves Ground **C**, where a surfaced footpath doubles back steeply on the left. This leads up to a metal gate;

Torver Low Common

through this, go left through another gate to gain a rising stony path beside a wall. Stay beside the wall when the track divides and soon pass through another gate giving onto rough moorland pasture.

Follow the path as it swings to the right and climbs across a hillside. The way out onto the commons is a quite delightful broad track, for the most part to the left of a wall. After passing beyond the end of the wall, the track swings left into an elongated valley, through the middle of which runs Mere Beck. Go left for a short distance but then descend into the middle of the valley keeping well to the left of an isolated and rather straggly, stunted tree **D**. Mere Beck turns out to be a mere beck, but the ground either side of it is frequently boggy.

On the other side, make for an obvious gully lined with juniper bushes and one large yew tree. Having climbed the gully, you pop out onto higher ground, which brings Torver Tarn into view beyond the whole spread of Torver Low Common. There are pathways here, all narrow trods through grass and easy to confuse with sheep tracks. So, your next objective is a substantial and solitary pine tree, with a few low-lying juniper tucked into a hollow nearby.

The path continues past the juniper bushes and then cuts across a low shoulder eventually to merge with the Cumbria Way **E**, which has here descended from Beacon Tarn *(see Walk 7)*. Now follow this out until it reaches a minor road. When you do reach the road, turn left and walk up to a signpost about 100 yds before reaching a wall. *(There is a variant finish here, that takes you up to the wall, there turning left to follow it all the way across Coats Hill and above Tyson Wood to reach the Torver road at Sunny Bank, from where it is a short uphill walk back to the start.)*

Leave the road and branch left onto a bridleway. When the track divides, it matters not which route you take – high or low – as both paths later rejoin. Torver Tarn is in view ahead, lying in a moorland hollow.

At a waymark, go left to another waymark at a stream crossing. The path on the other side takes you on to meet up with your outward route **A**. Here, simply branch right in order to retrace your steps. ●

Tarn Hows Wood and Yewdale

		GPS waypoints	
Start	Coniston		SD 304 975
Distance	5½ miles (9km)	A	SD 319 984
Height gain	885 feet (270m)	B	SD 330 994
Approximate time	2½ hours	C	SD 320 998
Parking	Coniston (Pay and Display)	D	SD 300 980
Route terrain	Woodland paths; some roadside walking		
Ordnance Survey maps	Landranger 97 (Kendal & Morecambe), Explorer OL7 (The English Lakes – South-eastern area)		

There is terrible temptation to visit Tarn Hows by driving there, parking up and doing a quick tour of the lake. But this walk sets off from the village of Coniston, and climbs steadily throughout the sylvan beauty of Tarn Hows Wood, touches briefly on the tarn edge, and then descends to the woodlands of Tom Gill and Yewdale. Whether you add the walk around the lake is for you to decide.

Set off from the car park near the tourist information centre in Coniston by turning right (ignoring the immediate street) onto a road that leads out of the village. After crossing the bridge spanning Yewdale Beck, move onto a sheltered footpath on the left-hand side of the road. You re-emerge on the road at the **Waterhead Hotel**.

Continue at the roadside, and shortly reach the edge of Coniston Water. Go past the turning to Brantwood, and keep on past Boon Crag Farm, and soon pass Monk Coniston Hall, high up on the right.

Monk Coniston is a neo-Gothic house leased from the National Trust by HF Holidays. The grounds contain a rare tree collection, and the estate was once owned by Beatrix Potter. Legend has it that Monk Coniston was built originally in the 13th century by the monks of Furness Abbey as a base from which to administer the lands they owned in this area. A building with such a purpose, Hawkshead Court House, just north of Hawkshead, does exist, but there seems to be no conclusive evidence for a similar building at Monk Coniston site.

After crossing a footbridge, you enter the lower edge of Tarn Hows Wood A. Cross a lane, and go forward onto an ascending gravel track into woodland. The track climbs steadily, and rises to intercept another track. Here keep left, briefly on the level, before climbing again. When the track forks, keep right for the Old Car Park, climbing steadily to the top edge of the woodland.

At the top of the climb, go through a gate onto a lane B. Turn left, towards Tarn Hows. You now have a number of choices. Your next objective is a gate at the near left-hand corner of Tarn Hows, where it outflows into Tom Gill. The road will lead you close to it, but there are a number of other footpaths that you can use just as effectively.

Follow the paths round to the gate, and having passed through it and crossed the top of Tom Gill, turn left onto a path that runs down the true right bank of the gill. *The path is steep in a few short places, and requires care as the rocks are slippery when wet.* Lower down you pass a neat waterfall, Tom Gill Force, beyond which the path leads steadily down to Glen Mary Bridge at the roadside.

Walk past the car park, but after about 50 yds, go left over a footbridge and into a sloping field. Keep right around the field edge and follow it to another gate **C** giving back onto the road. Turn right for a few strides and then left towards Yew Tree Farm. Almost immediately leave the farm access for a bridlegate on the right, giving onto a gravel path that climbs behind the farm.

When the track forks, keep left and follow the gravel path until it eventually emerges onto the Hodge Close lane at the single-arched Shepherd's Bridge. Cross the bridge, and on the other side, bear right onto a bridleway for Coniston. The path soon

runs alongside the Coniston road as it enters Yewdale woods. Cross the Tilberthwaite road, and then enjoy the lovely walk through the roadside woodlands and passing the quite spectacular spill of White Gill waterfall.

Keep following the track, and when it forks within a few strides of the road, bear right up to a gate in the intake wall. Now stay with the path beside the

Tarn Hows

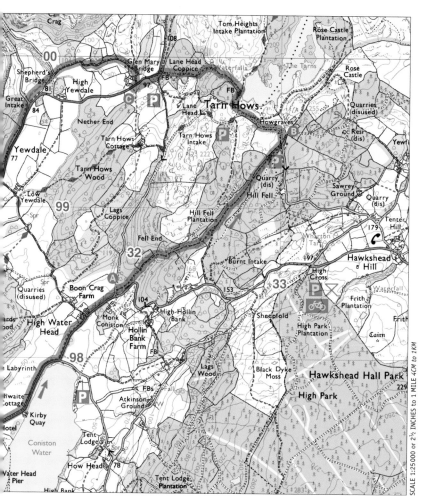

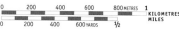

SCALE 1:25000 or 2½ INCHES to 1 MILE 4CM to 1KM

| 0 | 200 | 400 | 600 | 800 METRES | 1 |
| KILOMETRES |
| MILES |
| 0 | 200 | 400 | 600 YARDS | ½ |

wall. At the next gate you join a rough track that leads right up into Coppermines Valley. Here, turn left , and walk down into Coniston village. On the way you pass the Ruskin Museum – there has been a Ruskin Museum in Coniston since 1901. In 1999, the museum was extended, and is commonly regarded as one of the finest museums in the Lake District *(see page 95 for details)*. Eventually come out in the centre of the village at the **Black Bull Inn**. Turn right and walk past the **Yewdale Hotel**, and then immediately turn left to return to the car park. As you return to the start, you pass St Andrew's Church in the graveyard of

which lies John Ruskin, one of the greatest figures of the Victorian age: poet, artist, critic, social revolutionary, conservationist and from 1869 Slade Professor of Fine Art at Oxford University. Ruskin lived for the last 30 years of his life at Brantwood, on the far side of the lake. Upon his death, he was buried here in Coniston, and his grave marked by a large carved cross made from green slate quarried from nearby Tilberthwaite and designed by his friend and secretary W. G. Collingwood.

Seathwaite Tarn

		GPS waypoints
Start	Seathwaite	🥾 SD 229 962
Distance	4¾ miles (7.6km)	**A** SD 240 968
Height gain	1,065 feet (325m)	**B** SD 245 982
Approximate time	2½ hours	**C** SD 237 977
Parking	Roadside parking near Seathwaite church	
Route terrain	Fell moorland; woodland; farmland; some road walking	
Ordnance Survey maps	Landranger 96 (Barrow-in-Furness & South Lakeland), Explorer OL6 (The English Lakes – South-western area)	

Reposing beneath the steep slopes of Grey Friar near the head of the Duddon Valley, Seathwaite Tarn lies in a most profound location, one with a capacity to absorb a disproportionate amount of time doing nothing. The Duddon Valley itself, known as Dunnerdale, is a little-frequented part of the region as narrow, twisting roads deter visitors. Only the determined and the curious seek out Dunnerdale rewards, and there are many. Seathwaite Tarn is one of them. The walk starts from a parking area beside the River Duddon, just behind the church.

The name Seathwaite derives from a combination of the old Norse words *sef* (sedges) and *thveit* (later anglicised to 'thwaite', meaning a clearing) and may be taken to mean a clearing among the sedges. The name, then written Seuthwayt, first appeared in records dating from 1340.

A notable treasure of Seathwaite, not far from the start of the walk, is the **Newfield Inn**, a pub that dates from the packhorse days of the 16th century, and was visited by Wordsworth on his tours of the Lake District. The pub's most unusual feature is its banded slate floor, a product of the time when slate was easily gained and plentiful.

The Church of the Holy Trinity was built in the early 1500s, but has seen much restoration. Wordsworth visited the church and dedicated one of his *Duddon Sonnets* to the place and to the Reverend Robert Walker (1709-1802) who was parson here for 66 years. The church contains a memorial plaque to Walker, who was known as 'Wonderful Walker' because of his long and exemplary ministry. Wordsworth refers to him in the sonnet as '... a Gospel Teacher ... whose good works formed an endless retinue'. Prior to the inn opening, the Reverend Walker even brewed and sold his own ale *(see Walk 11)*.

🥾 Turn left up the road beside the bubbling Duddon, a watercourse of bright turquoise plunge pools and foaming cascades surrounded by trees favoured by red squirrels.

After about 440 yds, leave the road by turning right towards Turner Hall

Farm. As you approach the farm, go forward through a gate for High Moss and follow a broad track around the farm and on across fields to High Moss.

The summits directly in front of you are part of the Dow Crag ridge, extending south to White Maiden; you can pick out the course of the Walna Scar Road crossing the slopes of the fells.

At High Moss, keep to the left of the buildings to locate a gate giving into a rough pasture. Cross this to a narrow lane. Turn right and walk past Beck House; if you look half-left you will now see a slanting rake leading off to the northern skyline. This is the way the route is going.

When you reach a bridge  spanning Long House Gill, where the Walna Scar Road begins its upward journey, turn left over the bridge onto a superb service track rising at an easy gradient and leading all the way to Seathwaite Tarn. Prominent in view to the left is the pyramidal Harter Fell, and, perhaps less obviously, through a gap in the fells Scafell and Slight Side loom.

Once the track levels, as it nears the tarn, you pass a low waymark on the left ; note this for the return stage. Continue along the track with the great bulk of Grey Friar now putting in an appearance. The beauty of this approach to the tarn is that you do not see the lake until virtually the last moment, and that is heralded by the appearance of the dam wall. When you

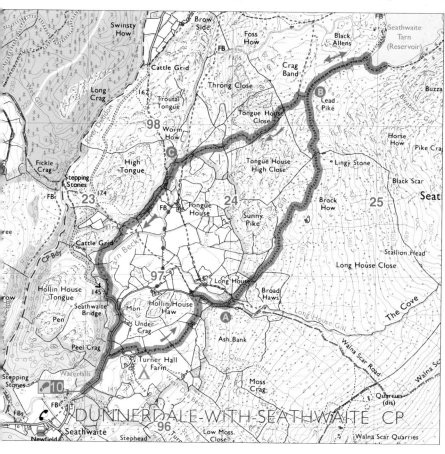

Seathwaite Tarn and Grey Friar

arrive at the tarn base, turn up to the right for a lovely view across the water; there is a path all the way round the tarn, but this is often marshy at the far end and a worthy compromise is either to remain near the dam or to walk a little farther to a prominent rise, which proves to be an excellent vantage point. Seathwaite Tarn was dammed in the 1930s to provide drinking water for Barrow-in-Furness. Its setting in a grand mountain hollow is superb, and the waters of the tarn are deep and shelve quickly.

Return by the upward route, as far as that low waymark, and there branch right on a clear footpath that wanders downwards in a most agreeable fashion through a series of rock outcrops and boulders, and later accompanies a stream, which at some point you need to step across to continue the descent. Eventually, the descent moves away from the stream, but the path is clear throughout and leads down to a gate as it enters the valley bottom. Keep following the path to another gate, after which you bear right to a ladder-stile,

then crossing Tarn Beck by a footbridge 🅒. On the other side, go half-left to a gate giving onto a path along the base of a wooded slope, and on the true right bank of Tarn Bank, which, alas, soon changes direction.

Keep to the right of a barn and cottage and then continue along the base of wooded slopes and beside a moss-covered wall. Just on passing a long, low barn the track bears off to the right, but keep an eye open for a path bearing left down from the main track to run alongside a fence. You can follow the main track if you wish, and it will lead you out to a road, but this gives you more road walking to complete the walk than necessary. *Instead, keep along the fence to a gate, and then by a path around a marshy area, with a few duckboards in place, and head out to meet a bridge spanning the Duddon.*

Turn left and cross the bridge, and then pass a road turning for Coniston, and farm access lanes to Under Crag and then Turner Hall beyond which you simply stroll down the road to complete the walk. ●

Dunnerdale Fells

		GPS waypoints
Start	Ulpha	
Distance	5 miles (8km)	🖉 SD 199 920
Height gain	1,395 feet (425m)	Ⓐ SD 197 929
Approximate time	2½ hours	Ⓑ SD 214 933
Parking	Along minor road	Ⓒ SD 216 928
		Ⓓ SD 219 912
Route terrain	Rugged going with numerous undulations, and rough conditions underfoot	
Ordnance Survey maps	Landranger 96 (Barrow-in-Furness & South Lakeland), Explorer OL6 (The English Lakes – South-western area)	

Ulpha is a scattered community nestling below the shapely fell called simply The Pike and astride the River Duddon. Its name means 'the enclosure where wolves are trapped', or 'Wolf's Hill', from Old Scandinavian. There are many undulations on this walk, with three principal climbs and descents, and, in spite of its brevity, it is quite demanding. It is also a walk that passes through a tranquil corner of Lakeland that few visitors ever reach.

🖉 Set off northwards along the road towards Ulpha, finally leaving the road just past the turning to Whistling Green by branching right onto a broad track, a bridleway (signposted for Kiln Bank) Ⓐ.

At the beginning of the 14th century, a deer park was made at Ulpha by one of the lords of Millom, and a fragment of the park still exists among the wooded hummocks below Ulpha. Hunting took place across all the rounded fells to the west, served by Frith Hall, which was built in the 15th century as a hunting lodge.

The Kiln Bank track is surfaced initially. Follow it as far as Low Birks, and there leave it for a steep path ascending on the right to thread a way through numerous rocky outcrops as it climbs steadily. A green path leads on through bracken and gorse, and provides a lovely view northwards along the valley to Harter Fell and the high fells of central Lakeland beyond.

Below Harter Fell, the valley changes direction at Cockley Beck bridge, where the Duddon heads south. This is the 'Dundale', mentioned frequently but never described in Arthur Ransome's novels. The river was said by Wordsworth to be his favourite, a place he came to fish during his schooldays in Hawkshead, and which inspired an entire series of sonnets – *The River Duddon* – which he wrote in 1820.

North of Ulpha, the Duddon tumbles through gorges green and lush, to Seathwaite, another small hamlet containing several houses, a parish church and an inn. The church was the domain of the Reverend Robert Walker (1709-1802), who gained some notoriety as a formidable man in more ways than one. Known to Wordsworth as 'wonderful Walker', he was born in Seathwaite in the 18th century and later preached at the parish church for over 60 years, and also taught local children. He was a painfully frugal man, but remarkable for his generosity and goodness, and in spite of a very low stipend of five pounds per year managed to leave over £2,000 in his will. His character and constitution enabled him to augment his stipend by ploughing fields, spinning cloth, and writing letters for those who could not read or write. He also availed himself of a number of local customs known as clog-shoes, harden-sark, whittle-gate and goose-gate, which gave a man in his position the right to claim shoes, clothing, food and lodging from the parish, as well as grazing on the common for his geese.

As you progress through the maze of low crags, the shapely cone of Caw springs into view, a minor fell that featured in Richard Adam's book *The Plague Dogs*. The track leads on to cross Hollow Moss Beck beyond which rises the craggy fell of Stickle Pike. Once across the beck the potential for confusion rises a notch or two, and it is easy to miss the correct line, as a multiplicity of paths testify. The main route gradually works a way across to the high point of a minor road at the head of a minor dale containing Dunnerdale Beck. *The failsafe, should you miss this, is a wall across the northern shoulder of the fells which, kept on your left with Caw always ahead, will guide you to the road, reaching it near a cattle-grid, from which all you need to do is climb the short distance to the high point of the road* Ⓑ *at Kiln Bank Cross.* Energetic walkers could do worse than scamper up nearby Stickle Pike; the view is superb and the short ascent nothing like as arduous as it seems from below. The hidden Stickle Tarn is a lovely place to rest and enjoy lunch.

From Kiln Bank Cross, descend towards the farm buildings at Hoses, passing through an area that was once quarried, and, lower down, ignore a distinct branching path climbing on the right. Instead, walk down to Hoses, and just on reaching a road gate Ⓒ, climb above a wall on the right to gain a path,

Dunnerdale Fells

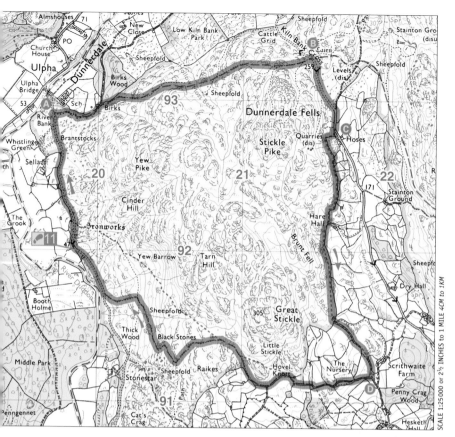

which then climbs steeply beside a wall. From a wall corner, go left above the intake wall and now descending.

The path accompanies the wall for some distance, eventually bringing the Duddon Estuary into view. The wall is, in fact, a good guide as it leads you past Hare Hall, crossing Hare Hall Beck and, later, Red Moss Beck beyond which a metal gate gives into an old walled track.

Go up the track briefly, and then follow its descending course to reach a point above Scrithwaite Farm. Just beyond, you intercept a broad grassy track, a bridleway **D**. Turn right onto this to enter another walled section rising gently. As the track levels so the fells surrounding Great Stickle come into view.

Continue beyond a gate where the track levels a little as it approaches a field barn, from where it once more climbs, to another gate, then going left alongside the intake wall to pass below Great Stickle.

When the accompanying wall changes direction, leave it and continue ascending on a grassy track through bracken to a col ahead where the ongoing path forks. Here branch left and immediately start losing height. When the track again divides below a small outcrop, branch right and soon begin descending more steeply, with the valley road now in view. As the ongoing path branches and bends left towards the road, go with it, and on reaching the road, turn right to complete the walk.

●

Eskdale Moor and Burnmoor Tarn

		GPS waypoints
Start	Dalegarth, Eskdale	
Distance	5¼ miles (8.5km)	🖉 NY 173 007
Height gain	935 feet (285m)	Ⓐ NY 176 018
		Ⓑ NY 174 025
Approximate time	2½ hours	Ⓒ NY 184 040
Parking	Dalegarth Station	Ⓓ NY 187 037
Route terrain	Moorland tracks; *not advised in poor visibility*	
Ordnance Survey maps	Landranger 89 (West Cumbria), Explorer OL6 (The English Lakes – South-western area)	

For a walk on the wild side there is nothing better than this romp across Eskdale Moor to Burnmoor Tarn, but it is not one to be contemplated in less than perfect visibility. *Legend tells that the moors are haunted by the spirit of a horse which bolted whilst conveying a corpse from Wasdale to Eskdale; they are also the happy hunting grounds of Bronze Age man, as stone circles on Brat's Moss testify.*

🖉 Start from the car park at Dalegarth Station, and walk left along the road towards Boot. Take the first turning on the left, at the **Brook House Inn**, onto a side lane for the **Watermill Inn**. As you walk along the lane, notice the dry-stone walls of Eskdale granite on either side; they are of considerable and unusual width and almost certainly built from stone cleared from adjacent fields.

Keep on through the village, cross a bridge next to Eskdale Corn Mill and pass Mill Cottage to go forward up a stony track to a gate. Turn right on a steeply ascending bridleway that zigzags between walls. As you reach the open moor, so you find a group of stone buildings Ⓐ that probably served as peat houses in which peat from the moor was dried and stored.

Stay on the path that runs past the buildings, and follow it out across the moor. *The way across the moor is continuous and intermittently cairned, but this is still no place to be in poor visibility.*

As the path climbs onto Brat's Moss you come to a low waymark pole Ⓑ, where the route bears right to pass below the obvious rise of Boat How. (From the pole it is easy, if you wish, to take a track on the left that leads to one of the stone circles, with more nearby.)

Take the clear track passing Boat How, after which it rises to the high point of the moor and begins a steady descent that brings Burnmoor Tarn into view. As you descend, the track forks: the left fork takes you directly to Burnmoor Lodge, while the main track maintains the original direction.

Burnmoor Tarn is one of the largest

tarns in Lakeland, and the lodge an indication that it is popular with anglers. The tarn lies in a wide hollow crossed by an old corpse road, and is a remarkably evocative and peaceful place to be, in the middle of nowhere, surrounded by so much emptiness and open space, where the flight of moorland birds give shape to the wind, and their song is a melody played on the finest of Nature's instruments.

The key to the return leg is Lambford Bridge, spanning Whillan Beck. To locate it you need to keep an eye open for a path arriving from Burnmoor Lodge on the left **C**. Where the paths intercept, there is another path heading right, at 90°. This, occasionally uncertain path, does lead directly to Lambford Bridge **D**, below the crags of Eskdale Fell.

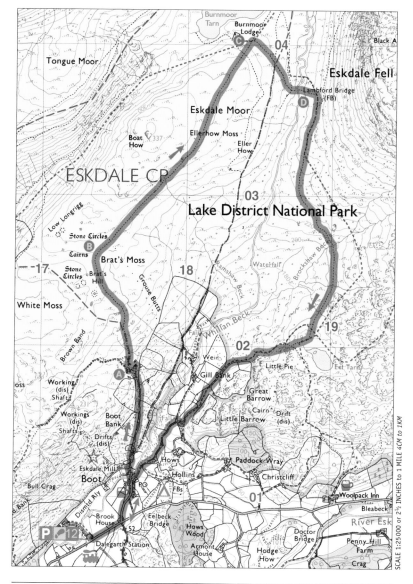

SCALE 1:25 000 or 2 ½ INCHES to 1 MILE 4CM to 1KM

On the other side of the bridge, a clear path swings right (southwards), and is generally clear and continuous, but subject to minor bouts of uncertainty. The objective, Eel Tarn, however, is in view from the early stages of this return track. This is a superb moorland tramp, with a fine sense of openness and freedom, and grassy underfoot. The track passes north of Eel Tarn, but it is an easy undertaking to divert up to view the tarn before returning to the original line.

Eventually the ongoing track is funnelled between walls, and leads past Gill Bank Farm, the grounds of which house a Chilean pine tree, a strange sight in so remote a setting. Stay parallel with the wall on the right, and when the track forks, bear right down to a three-way signpost. Turn right through a gate, and then left down the access track to Gill Bank. The track soon becomes surfaced and leads directly down into Boot. Turn left to walk out to the valley road, and there head right, to complete the walk at Dalegarth Station. ●

Stone circle, Brat's Moss

Top o'Selside and Arnsbarrow Hill

		GPS waypoints
Start	High Nibthwaite	
Distance	6 miles (9.5km)	SD 296 909
Height gain	1,245 feet (380m)	Ⓐ SD 294 897
		Ⓑ SD 303 917
Approximate time	3 hours	Ⓒ SD 310 912
Parking	Car park north of High Nibthwaite (limited roadside parking near Water Park)	Ⓓ SD 304 899
Route terrain	Rough fell paths and tracks; confusing terrain – *not advised in poor visibility*	
Ordnance Survey maps	Landranger 96 (Barrow-in-Furness & South Lakeland), Explorers OL6 (The English Lakes – South-western area) and OL7 (The English Lakes – South-eastern area)	

This walk is not for days of poor visibility without exceptional navigational skills. *At other times this is a splendid chance to practise finding your way by reading the terrain, which is hummocky, heathery, boggy, craggy and convoluted, opening up new vistas at almost every step and inviting confusion. The heights of Bethecar Moor – Top o'Selside and Arnsbarrow Hill – are seldom visited, but the view across Coniston Water to the Coniston Fells is outstanding. The comparative isolation and peace makes this a habitat that is ideal for adders; so take care where you put your feet.*

The car park north of Nibthwaite requires almost one mile of road walking to reach the hamlet; fortunately the views it affords of Coniston Water and the fells beyond make it worthwhile. In Nibthwaite leave the road for a lane Ⓐ between buildings (after the post box and before the telephone box) that leads briefly to a gate giving on to a stony track that provides the first stage of the walk.

The track is straightforward, alternately ascending and then level as it cuts a swathe across bracken slopes dotted with heather, juniper and gorse. As you climb, there is an improving view of the Coniston Fells.

The mini cascades of Selside Beck inject a moment's frivolity, but as you pass the top of the beck, the track swings left and eventually breaks free of accompanying walls, and runs on across open fellside.

Below, at the edge of Coniston Water is Peel Island, a small tree-draped tuffet anchored at the water's edge, formerly known as Montagu Island, and gifted to the National Trust in 1932 by the seventh Duke of Buccleuch, John Charles Montagu Douglas Scott, a Scottish member of Parliament. Today,

Selside Beck

relates to the east summit.

Close by is Arnsbarrow Tarn, an almost circular splash of water trapped by the moraines of two retreating glaciers. In the 14th century, this jumble-land of bog and tussocky mayhem was populated by lawless brigands led by the notorious Adam de Beaumont, who devolved a reign of terror on the surrounding countryside for the 17 years it took the authorities, such as they were, to capture him.

South-east from Top o'Selside, Arnsbarrow Hill is the next objective. Any attempt to take a direct route will flounder in quagmire either side of Tarn Beck. What is important to keep in mind is that from leaving the main trail at Ⓑ, the path across the whole of this walk is continuous; you may not find it amid all the sheep tracks, but it is there.

the island is better known as the inspiration, probably along with Blakeholme in Windermere, for Arthur Ransome's 'Wildcat Island' portrayed in *Swallows and Amazons*, originally published in 1930. The island also features in a novel – *Thorstein of the Mere, A Saga of the Northmen in Lakeland* – by W. G. Collingwood, some-time secretary of art critic, social thinker, author, poet and artist, John Ruskin.

Keep climbing along the track to reach a high point at a waymark Ⓑ, and here leave the track and turn right onto an ascending grassy path that soon divides. Branch left to walk up to the summit of Top o'Selside, marked by a large cairn. Top o'Selside cairn is a fitting place to have a quiet dither about whether the cairned top or the unmarked one a short distance away to the east is the higher. This seeming irrelevance is of particular importance to list tickers, for Top o'Selside is a Marilyn. GPS readings show the cairned summit, at 332m, to be 2m higher than the east, although neither height matches that on the OS map (335m), which height, just to confuse matters,

The path loops around the northern part of the tarn, and then sets about easing up onto Arnsbarrow Hill Ⓒ, never quite touching on the summit, to which a deviation would be necessary. Before reaching the southernmost high point of Arnsbarrow Hill (316m), the path dives to the right (south-west), and runs steeply down across Stang Moss towards High Light Haw. But before reaching this isolated craggy mound you intercept a more pronounced path that originated just to the east of point Ⓑ.

Once you reach this path, turn left onto it and follow it roughly southwards. Just before it reaches a wall, the path divides. Take the right branch and walk on to the wall, crossed by a step-stile Ⓓ, just north of High Bethecar Farm. However, there is no need to cross the stile. Instead, keep to the right of a wall, following a path for Nibthwaite. It later joins the High Bethecar path. Keep to the right of the wall, and soon descend to cross Caws Beck, and continue on the other side through bracken, and all the while now

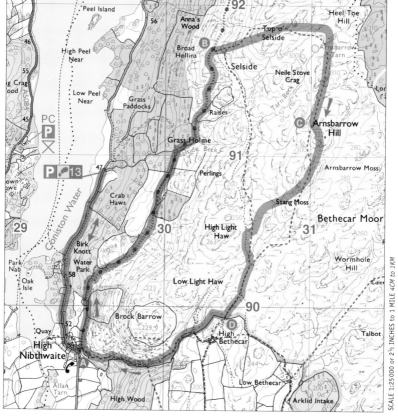

steadily descending.

The path is no longer in doubt, and brings you down in quite splendid fashion to return to the road at Nibthwaite, from where it is a simple matter to return to your starting point. ●

Coniston Water at Nibthwaite

Greendale Tarn, Seatallan
and Middle Fell

		GPS waypoints
Start	Greendale	
Distance	5 miles (8km)	📝 NY 144 056
Height gain	2,460 feet (750m)	Ⓐ NY 143 064
Approximate time	3 hours	Ⓑ NY 147 081
Parking	Off-road parking at start	
Route terrain	Steep start through a rocky ravine with two fairly *steep climbs,* on to Seatallan *(optional)* and Middle Fell; *rocky descent*	
Ordnance Survey maps	Landranger 89 (West Cumbria), Explorer OL6 (The English Lakes – South-western area)	

The craggy flanks of Buckbarrow and Middle Fell are much in evidence from the back roads around Nether Wasdale, but behind their bold front the grassy spread of Nether Wasdale Common (rising to its highest point on Seatallan) and the beautifully sited Greendale Tarn, are out of sight and seldom visited. It is the apparent shapelessness of Seatallan that perhaps deters many walkers, but this tour of Greendale, Seatallan and the adjoining minor top, Middle Fell, will be found to be one of many delights, and quite a few surprises.

Red Pike seen over Nether Beck

📝 From the grass and bracken beside the road at Greendale, a clear path sets off towards an obvious gully down which Greendale Gill displays a number of attractive cascades. A little steepness starts the day, but this relents a touch as a corner is rounded where you gain a better view of the gill. From the corner, a narrow path may be seen soaring upwards on to Middle Fell, and it is by this way that the walk concludes.

Meanwhile, continue along the path above the true left bank of the gill, with both the path and gill meeting at a narrowing of the ravine, a perfect place for a breather. Quite a few streams feed into the gill at this point, hence the name Tongues Gills Ⓐ.

Continue with the line of Greendale Gill, and, as the gradient collapses completely, so the inspiring cliffs of Middle Fell come into view, opposing the gentler grassy flank of Seatallan. At any time you can cross the gill and set off up the slopes of Seatallan, but there is greater merit in continuing to Greendale Tarn, concealed until the last moment by a small morainic plug.

Though much less than an hour's walk from civilisation, beside this peaceful tarn you could be in another world. It takes a determined effort to raise yourself to cross the gill, or walk round to the northern end of the tarn and up to a broad boggy col 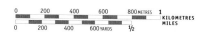 to tackle the slopes of Seatallan, although this extension is optional. There is no significant path to follow, simply an instinct for the easiest line, and this will lead you on to the vast summit plateau, at the northern end of which a trig overlooking Blengdale marks the highest point. The large mound of stones on the summit is thought to be an ancient tumulus.

From Seatallan, if you descend south of east you will come to the broad col 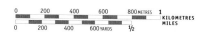 with adjoining Middle Fell, across which a path materialises, and rises through a much rockier landscape, dotted with small bright-eyed tarns, to the top of Middle Fell. The path is cairned from above the col, though it is never in doubt, and provides excellent views of the hinterland of the ancient Copeland Forest – Haycock, Scoat Fell and Red Pike, against which Scoat

Tarn and Low Tarn rest darkly.

The path continues over the top of Middle Fell, and descends through numerous rock outcrops, easily avoiding difficulties. Lower down, good views appear of the screes spilling into Wastwater from Illgill Head, against which the bright greens of the valley pastures make a vibrant contrast.

Gradually the descending path brings you back to the path corner noticed on the ascent, from where your outward steps are easily retraced. ●

SCALE 1:25 000 or 2½ INCHES to 1 MILE 4CM to 1KM

Caw

		GPS waypoints	
Start	Seathwaite	 SD 229 962	
Distance	5¼ miles (8.2km)	Ⓐ SD 223 947	
Height gain	1,755 feet (535m)	Ⓑ SD 228 948	
Approximate time	3 hours	Ⓒ SD 243 948	
Parking	Roadside parking near Seathwaite church	Ⓓ SD 248 964	
Route terrain	Rough fell tracks; old quarry workings; craggy moorland		
Ordnance Survey maps	Landranger 96 (Barrow-in-Furness & South Lakeland), Explorer OL6 (The English Lakes – South-western area)		

Wherever you are in that delectable hinterland of low fells west of Coniston, Caw somehow muscles in on the act, its prominence a perfect example of how small is beautiful. There is an approach from Kiln Bank Cross to the south west, which reduces the ascent, but this climb from Seathwaite facilitates a return via the Walna Scar Road.

Begin from the roadside parking area behind Seathwaite church *(see Walk 10 for more information about the church and the village),* and turn right to walk down towards the **Newfield Inn**. Leave the road just before the inn, by branching left through gated sheep-folds onto a rough track, Park Head Road, climbing close to Old Park Beck.

Continue up this old miner's track for a little over ¾ mile until you locate an old stone-bordered incline branching off to the left Ⓐ. With close-cropped turf underfoot, stride up this incline to a point where the remains of a tooling shed and spoil heaps mark the end of the track Ⓑ. *Nearby a mine level is approached by a lovely path, but should really be avoided, as these old workings are generally unstable and dangerous.*

There is an indistinct path upwards now, keeping to the left of a stream, later crossing it, and rising almost to the skyline above. With height a clearer path emerges and this leads you left, up to the summit, crowned by a trig pillar, and rewarding the effort with a spectacular view reaching to the very heart of Lakeland with Crinkle Crags, Bowfell, Esk Pike and the Scafells clearly in sight.

There is much merit in now retreating

Caw from Frith Hall, Ulpha Park

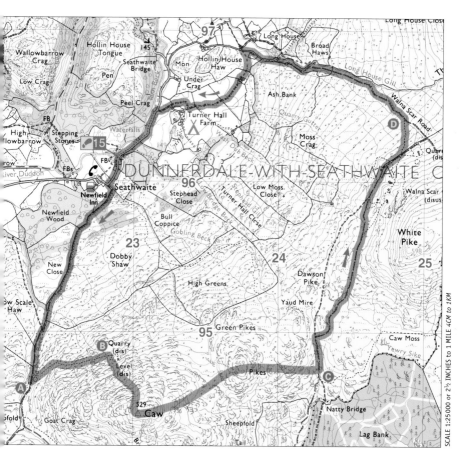

SCALE 1:25000 or 2½ INCHES to 1 MILE 4CM to 1KM

by your outward route, and retracing your steps to Seathwaite. The continuation, however, makes for the low hillock to the east, Pikes, and involves some rough ground and a few minor navigational issues. There is a path across the intervening ground, some of which is marshy, but the objective is clear enough.

Beyond Pikes you continue eastwards, descending through rocky and bouldery terrain until you intercept a bridleway **C**. Here, turn left (roughly north) and follow the track across the western slopes of White Pike, enjoying expansive views of the upper Duddon Valley. The track eventually closes in on the prominent line of the Walna Scar Road to which a shortcut descends **D**.

Now simply follow the track downwards to reach the end of a surfaced lane, close by a bridge spanning Long House Gill. Walk down the road and soon pass Beck House. A short way farther on, turn through a gate onto a path across rough pasture that leads to another gate and emerges at the rear of High Moss Farm. Take a path to the right of the farm and then follow a wide field track across two pastures towards Turner Hall Farm. As you approach the farm, the track swings to the right to pass around it, and comes to a gate.

Keep forward along an access drive and soon reach the valley road. Turn left to return to Seathwaite. ●

Coniston Old Man

		GPS waypoints
Start	Coniston	 SD 304 975
Distance	5 miles (8km)	**A** SD 285 981
Height gain	2,430 feet (740m)	**B** SD 276 982
Approximate time	3 hours	
Parking	Coniston (Pay and Display)	
Route terrain	A rocky trail, on clear paths. *Parts can be confusing in mist, and the summit trig is very close to a steep drop*	
Ordnance Survey maps	Landranger 97 (Kendal & Morecambe), Explorer OL6 (The English Lakes – South-western area)	

The ascent begins along Church Beck before climbing through old quarries to reach Low Water and a final haul to the summit; it's a slaty way, and strewn with the remnant produce of man's industry. But when you reach the summit of the fell, there is a fine sensation of other-worldliness and achievement that reduces the spoil of toil to its rightful place in history, a brief passage of time. Nothing can detract from the wellbeing of conquering the Old Man.

From the main car park in Coniston, go left into the village and across the bridge, then immediately turning right along a minor road to the **Sun Hotel**. Here turn right onto a signposted path to the Old Man and Levers Water that pursues the course of Church Beck.

This pleasant start soon leads to a bridge at the entrance to Coppermines Valley. Keep left at this point, continuing on a less broad path and gaining height steadily as you rise to meet a well-constructed track at a bend **A**, just to the north of The Bell. Turn right, following the track as it twists upwards through increasingly rough terrain and the spoil of quarrying generations past. Only a keen industrial archaeologist would find the untidy scenes of turmoil and dereliction attractive, yet the many

tumbled piles of slate, the rusted machinery and defunct buildings, arouse curiosity, about the men who toiled here, the hardships they faced, and the many dangers.

Some of the dangers are still present, especially if you venture near the main quarry, a vast hollow hacked from the hill, but unseen from the main path. At the top of a rise the path bends left then right. *If, before turning right, you continue ahead, you encounter a vast cavern, created by quarrymen. It is very dangerous now, having suffered roof collapses in the recent past. Do not enter, under any circumstances.*

Return to the main path, and ascend to reach Low Water **B** reposing in an enormous cirque of cliffs and steep, unstable slopes. This is one of Lakeland's grandest settings, the hue of the water, tinted blue by copper, injecting brightness into the scene.

The top of the Old Man lies directly above, but to reach it you must follow a rough and steep path zigzagging across the south wall of this corrie. Once at the top, turn right, and follow a broad, shaly path to the summit. The trig pillar is in a commanding position overlooking the Low Water basin.

The Old Man of Coniston was first ascended in 1792 by Captain Joseph Budworth, who had already that day walked from Ambleside to Coniston, to see the lake, and found himself unable to resist the challenge of the fell. Sustained only by brandy, he completed the first recorded ascent, and still walked back to Ambleside.

The top of the mountain used to possess three stone beacons – 'the Old Man', his 'Wife', and 'Son', clear evidence that others had ventured here ahead of Budworth. The largest of the three had a small chamber that provided rudimentary shelter. The disappearance of the beacons, it is alleged, was occasioned by Ordnance Survey engineers.

The measured distances and height gain for this walk assume a return by the outward route; a sufficient and satisfying prospect, without needing to extend the day any further. *Those with time, energy and inclination to do so, can effect a more circuitous return by continuing briefly northwards from the Old Man, before descending, left, on a rough path, to reach Goat's Hause, north-east of Goat's Water. From this broad boggy col, you can either descend to Goat's Water and follow a good path out to the Walna Scar Road, or ascend Dow Crag, to follow the long, undulating ridge to the Walna Scar Pass.* ●

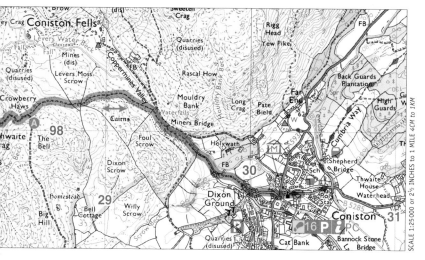

Dent and Kinniside Stone Circle

Dent and Kinniside Stone Circle

		GPS waypoints	
Start	Cleator Moor	🖊 NY 030 144	
Distance	7 miles (11km)	Ⓐ NY 023 134	
Height gain	1,575 feet (480m)	Ⓑ NY 027 135	
Approximate time	3½ hours	Ⓒ NY 055 130	
Parking	Roadside parking at Wath Bridge	Ⓓ NY 057 139	
Route terrain	Open fell tops and tracks; woodland tracks		
Ordnance Survey maps	Landranger 89 (West Cumbria), Explorer OL4 (The English Lakes – North-western area)		

The fell is a superb vantage point, showing what lies ahead for long-distance walkers with a come-hither-if-you-dare challenge that will unsettle a few. Closer to hand, lies one of the last unsung dales of Lakeland, Uldale. This walk takes a glimpse into the dale, before strolling through Nannycatch and up onto Blakeley Moss where there is a stone circle.

The key to the walk is the small town of Cleator Moor, historically linked with the iron works industry; the influx of Irish workers gave the town the nickname 'Little Ireland'. On the outskirts of town lies Wath Bridge – 'wath' being a Scandinavian word for a ford or crossing point. Today, there is a fine bridge, spanning the River Ehen, which has its source in Ennerdale Water.

🖊 Start from the nearby roadside parking and cross the bridge, turning immediately right onto a narrow side lane. You follow this lane, with good views to the west, towards the coast, for one mile, as far as Black How Plantation on the left Ⓐ, opposite a group of cottages. Here, leave the road and turn into the plantation, taking to a broad, gravel track rising into woodland. When you reach a junction Ⓑ, turn left for Dent Fell, and now following a narrow path along the edge of a larch plantation.

Kinniside Stone Circle

After about 100 yds, the path swings to the right, and climbs through a firebreak towards Dent Fell.

At the top of the plantation, cross a track, and go forward beside a fence, maintaining this direction onto the highest part of the fell. Optimism may lead you to hope that the prominent cairn you see ahead is the top of the fell. But reality shows it to be a shelter, with the very modest cairn that marks

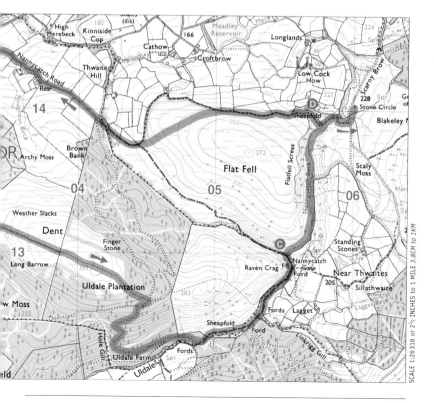

Wath Bridge, Cleator Moor

the true summit another 600 yds distant across a grassy summit plateau.

Just a few strides beyond the cairn, the path starts to descend. Cross a stile, and continue down through an area of cleared plantation to intercept a forest trail at a signpost. Turn right, and shortly meet another track. Cross this and go down along the edge of the plantation, with more cleared areas to the right. The descending track is steep in places, and requires care, but you get lovely cameos of Uldale framed by trees.

Eventually, the track merges with another running out from Uldale. Go forward along this to another junction, and here turn left, almost immediately leaving the broad trail for a bridleway on the left, passing through a gate, and then following a charming route through a simple dale, crossing and recrossing a stream in the process.

Follow the path until it reaches a gate and stile **C** (known as Nannycatch Gate), beyond which the path divides. Turn right, keeping east of Flat Fell, and when, just after crossing a small stream, the path divides, bear right past a low hillock. The path climbs towards the moorland road, but when it forks bear sharp right to go up to the road. The Kinniside Stone Circle lies a short

distance to the left, on the other side of the road.

Kinniside Stone Circle may be a bit of a sham, a modern creation, but one that is probably on or near the site of a prehistoric circle. A number of the original stones, were long ago taken for farming use, but in 1925 a restoration job was carried out by a Dr Quinn, using many of the original stones, which had been tracked down, recovered and set in concrete.

Having visited the stone circle, retrace your steps into Nannycatch Valley, but as you go back, instead of taking a lower path used earlier, stay on a slightly higher path **D** that curves round to the right into a western arm of the dale and feeds into a broad track, initially cobbled, and leading up onto the north side of Flat Fell.

The path accompanies a wall for some distance and then as both wall and path start to descend as you draw level with the western end of Meadley Reservoir to the north, move away from the wall, bearing left across the slope of Flat Fell. The path brings you down to the top end of Nannycatch Road, here a rough track. Turn right onto it; after a gate the road becomes surfaced and leads down to emerge on the valley road a short distance north east of Wath Bridge, and the completion of the walk. ●

Wast Water

		GPS waypoints	
Start	Wasdale		NY 151 054
Distance	8 miles (12.5km)	Ⓐ	NY 148 048
Height gain	740 feet (225m)	Ⓑ	NY 142 039
Approximate time	3½ hours	Ⓒ	NY 152 045
Parking	Numerous roadside parking areas and car parks		
Route terrain	Woodland paths; rugged and uneven tracks across boulder slopes; road walking		
Ordnance Survey maps	Landranger 89 (West Cumbria), Explorer OL6 (The English Lakes – South-western area)		

The remoteness of Wasdale is acutely inspirational: a heady tang of wild, uncut mountain gems that soar from valley sides with the air of majesty. At the head of the dale rise Kirk Fell, Great Gable and Lingmell, an iconic trio that compose the emblem of the Lake District National Park. With this assembly almost always in view, this walk takes a tour of the valley's lake, Wast Water, and offers the extremes of easy roadside walking in a superb setting and the most rugged test of footwear, balance and nerve across the infamous Wasdale screes.

There are numerous parking places along the length of Wasdale, some simple roadside pull-ins, others 'Pay and Display' or 'Honesty Box' parking areas. Where you start is irrelevant; it all depends on whether you want your road walking at the start or the end of your walk.

🥾 Set off in a south-westerly direction along the road, following it until, as it approaches the grounds of Wasdale Hall (now a youth hostel, and originally built in 1829), it swings to the right, away from the lake. Here, leave the road and locate a ladder-stile Ⓐ giving into light woodland, through which you follow a lakeside path towards the youth hostel. On the way, the path passes a perfectly placed bench from which to admire the view up the valley – on some days you may go no farther; it's all quite idyllic.

Beyond the youth hostel the lakeside path makes a loop around Low Wood, a small wooded hill, to reach a boat house, where the path now swings to the right in order to find a way that takes you to the building on the opposite shore; it's actually a pumping station.

When the path forks, bear left, and gradually you pass the end of the lake and take to the River Irt that flows from it (always a good quiz question). Eventually the path comes to a kissing-gate in a wall, just by Lund Bridge Ⓑ. Cross the bridge and follow a path going to the left to reach a service track to the pumping station. Turn left along this, and when you reach the building, keep to the right of it to begin the

traverse of Wast Water screes, which
sets off as a narrow path.

Now is a good time to take in
Wasdale. The lake is almost 3 miles
(4.5km) long, and ⅓ mile wide (700m);
it lies 215 ft (65m) above sea level, but
the bottom of the lake is more than
230ft (70m) down – below sea level.
This is one of the finest examples of a
glacially over-deepened valley. The
steep slopes on the south-eastern side of
the lake rise to the summits of Illgill
Head and Whin Rigg, perfectly
innocuous summits in their own right
viewed from the south, but with a
downfall of scree that is awesome. The
screes, which you are about to tread, were
formed as a result of ice and erosion,

0	200	400	600	800 METRES	1	
					KILOMETRES	
					MILES	
0	200	400	600 YARDS	½		

try as much as possible to maintain the same direction. If you arrive on the other side directly on the continuing path, you have done very well.

Once beyond the first main downfall, a path does then lead on. Subsequent downfalls are of smaller boulders, and a path becomes possible. After all the screes have been passed, a simple path leads out to Wasdale Head Hall Farm, and then Brackenclose, before finally crossing Lingmell Gill and the wider Lingmell Beck, where new bridge works have become necessary to accommodate the seasonal effects of this important water course. Three bridges have come and gone in the last 100 years at this point, necessitating the development of a river naturalisation scheme that will see bridge development work undertaken.

Over Lingmell Beck, you soon reach the valley road, and all that remains is to turn left and walk back to your starting point.   ●

Wast Water and the screes

and rise for over almost 2,000 ft (600m).

The scree has, however, been in situ for many, many years, and has amply stabilised. But it is vital to ensure the correct placement of feet, and not attempt to rush across. The larger boulders are more 'fixed' than the smaller, but as you cross the screes, an exhilarating experience, it is important that you relax and take your time. It is all very special: mildly intimidating, exhilarating, enthralling, energizing, thrilling and distinctly unique.

When you reach the first major downfall of scree ●, the path disappears: the boulders are large, and it is impossible for a path to be fashioned across them. The key is to keep between 10–15 yds above the water's edge, and to

Wetherlam

Start	High Tilberthwaite
Distance	5½ miles (8.8km)
Height gain	2,295 feet (700m)
Approximate time	3½ hours
Parking	At start
Route terrain	Rough fell slopes; *steep ascent and descent; the top of Wetherlam is confusing in mist*
Ordnance Survey maps	Landrangers 90 (Penrith & Keswick) and 96 (Barrow-in-Furness & South Lakeland), Explorer OL6 (The English Lakes – South-western area)

GPS waypoints

🖉	NY 306 010
Ⓐ	NY 304 007
Ⓑ	NY 293 016
Ⓒ	NY 287 011
Ⓓ	SD 293 990

A popular tourist place during Victorian times, Tilberthwaite Gill is a natural gorge of considerable beauty, through which flows Yewdale Beck, though the stream is generally known as Tilberthwaite Gill. The region also saw its share of slate quarrying during the 19th century. Overlording the gill, and a landscape that has notable appeal, rises Wetherlam, a fine, rugged, satisfying summit, here ascended from Tilberthwaite by a justifiably popular route.

The hamlet of Low Tilberthwaite lies secreted within enfolding fells, along a minor road that runs acutely away from the A593 about 1½ miles north of

Low Tilberthwaite

Coniston. Take care as you drive along this winding road – the scenery is a great distraction.

🖉 From the lower edge of a commodious (but in summer inadequate) car park a flight of slate steps ascends quickly through quarry spoil to a path junction. *On the way you pass Penny Rigg Quarry, which is worth a peek, but keep children and dogs under control since there are sudden and unfenced drops within the quarry.*

At the path junction Ⓐ you have a choice of ways. Either (a) go right, and descend to a bridge spanning Tilberthwaite Gill, and then steeply (on an unstable footpath) to join a former miners' track. Turn left. Or (b) climb left for a little pleasant cavorting with rocky knuckles *(slippery when wet)*, before the path opens out and swings round to head towards Crook Beck.

More evidence of quarrying now appears, in a vast mountain arena that is a fascinating place for the curious; but a dangerous one, too.

Slate quarrying has been a lasting source of wealth for the Lakeland economy, though inland quarries, like those above Tilberthwaite, had a limited period of prosperity, often supplying only a local market. Yet, as long ago as 1818, merchants, like Thomas Rigge of Hawkshead, were exporting Tilberthwaite green slate, carrying it via Coniston Water to Greenodd, from where it went by sloop to seaports throughout England and Ireland.

Pass through the quarrying area, *but do keep well away from shafts and adits.* By a footbridge, cross Tilberthwaite Gill, and climb to the miners' track joined earlier by walkers who chose to cross the gill lower down. Turn left along the track to begin a splendid, rising walk that visits the ruins of Hellen's Mine, and skirts the marshlands of Dry Cove, once flooded to provide power for a water wheel at the Tilberthwaite Mine, to arrive at the Borlase Mine, high above the cove.

Take a rough but enjoyable path,

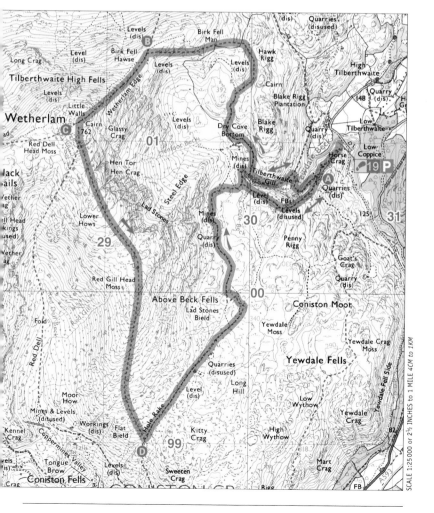

Coniston Water from Wetherlam

ascending right, in zigzags to reach Birk Fell Hawse ⑧, a narrow neck of land linking Wetherlam and nearby Birk Fell. This upper section of the walk, with its retrospective view of Dry Cove and the quarrylands beyond, is splendid; the arrival at Birk Fell Hawse, even better. For here, the ground falls, almost unnoticed, across Greenburn, before sprawling onwards across the fells above Langdale and out to the distant Scafells.

The ascent to the top of Wetherlam now pursues a fine, rocky (and, if you want it, scrambly) ridge, networked by paths, all of which guide you ever upwards. The top of the fell ⓒ is a vast rocky platform, with views as far-reaching as Ingleborough in Craven. Much nearer lies the Old Man of Coniston and Swirl How, separated by the modest hump of Brim Fell. Among the summit rocks there are many nooks in which to shelter, or you could press on towards a conspicuous cairn to the south (signalling the eventual way off), and then deviate to the right for a secluded break gazing across at the Old Man.

The cairn lies along a steadily improving path that descends for quite some distance through rocky knolls and tarn-filled hollows – a delightful experience – eventually to move left (south-east) to fall gradually to a path near the top of Hole Rake Pass ⓓ. Go left, along the path, passing a small reed-filled tarn, and continue, north-east and north, in the company of Crook Beck, until you ultimately return to the quarry site at the head of Tilberthwaite Gill.

You can return to the car park quickly by turning right, along the path on the south side of the gill, or, preferably, re-cross the footbridge ahead (used earlier in the walk), and turn right to reach the miners' track. Go right again, now descending the track, with Tilberthwaite Gill below on the right, and continue a pleasurable descent to a gate/wall just above Low Tilberthwaite.

Continue with the path, down and round to the cottages below, where you will find a fine example of a cottage with a spinning gallery, from which wool would be hung to dry.

On reaching the road, the car park remains only a few strides away to the right. ●

St Bees Head

		GPS waypoints	
Start	St Bees		NX 961 117
Distance	8 miles (13km)	Ⓐ	NX 949 151
Height gain	1,215 feet (370m)	Ⓑ	NX 968 149
Approximate time	4 hours	Ⓒ	NX 981 141
Parking	Beach promenade (Pay and Display)		
Route terrain	Rugged mountain tops and tracks; *not advised in poor visibility*		
Ordnance Survey maps	Landranger 89 (West Cumbria), Explorer 303 (Whitehaven & Workington)		

The sea cliffs of St Bees are a fabulous viewpoint with especial appeal for birdwatchers. Coincidentally, St Bees is the starting (or finishing point) of the Northern Coast-to-Coast Walk, which jaunts across the breadth of Britain to Robin Hood's Bay on the Yorkshire coast. The walk uses the 'C2C', as it is referred to, for the greater part of the route, but then bids it farewell as it makes an agreeable return to St Bees.

Set off by walking past the Lifeboat Station and on reaching the foreshore turn right around the edge of a caravan site to locate a footbridge giving onto a path rising onto South Head, also known as Tomlin. Not surprisingly, given the wealth of birdlife that appears (and breeds) along the sea cliffs in the course of a year, the whole area is an RSPB Nature Reserve.

St Bees South Head

The history of St Bees is fascinating and extensive. The village is said to owe its name to Bega, a 7th-century saint cast ashore at Fleswick Bay. The earliest records about St Bega come from the *Life and Miracles of St Bega the Virgin,* a manuscript now in the British Museum, and dating from the 12th century.

Tradition has it that on the day that Bega, the daughter of an Irish king, was supposed to be married to a Norse prince, she fled the court, and was transported by an angel to the

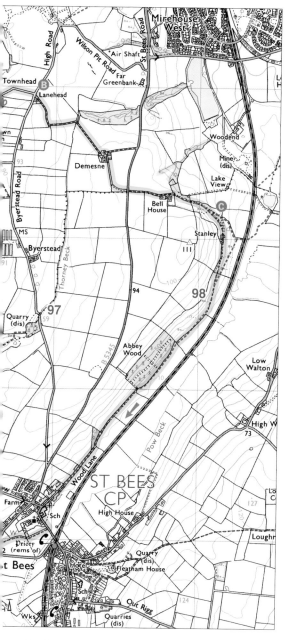

miracles happen, and the next day it snowed. The lord, true to his word, gave her the land and she went on to found a small nunnery that in time grew to become the powerful Priory of St Bees.

Present-day St Bees was not always so named. In the Henry VIII's *Valor Ecclesiasticus* of 1535, the village is identified as Kyrkeby Becok. When the priory was dissolved in 1539, the translation of its Latin name rendered it as the cell of St Bees. And St Bees it has been ever since.

The path across South Head is clear, *but does stray close to the sea cliffs in a way that may intimidate anyone without a head for heights*. To make things easier, you will find a couple of places where kissing-gates have been introduced into boundary fences to enable a route to be made that does not venture too close to the edge. In reality, the 'new' routes thus opened up are simply following the collapsed and largely buried course of ancient field boundaries.

Cumbrian coast. Here, recovered from her journey, she asked the local lord for land on which to build a nunnery. He replied dismissively that she could have as much land as was covered the next day by snow. He probably thought, it being midsummer at the time, that he had seen the last of the woman. But buried course of ancient field boundaries.

Along much of the route, gorse is abundant, imbuing the air with the heady scent of cinnamon. An old Second World War lookout station, built in 1938 and manned throughout the war, today invites a welcome breather.

Lighthouse, St Bees Head

The first indent to the clifftop route comes at Fleswick Bay, where you turn briefly inland to cross a ravine, and continue to climb onto North Head, adorned by a lighthouse. Here the path keeps to the landward side of a fence, again following the course of an old field boundary.

Continue past the lighthouse to find that the route takes a north-easterly direction, with Whitehaven now in view across Saltom Bay. Not long after passing a welcome bench, you also pass an old step-stile Ⓐ. Ignore this, and keep around the edge of a field, heading towards a nearby wall gap. Now keep the gorse-covered wall on your left and walk up-field to intercept a vehicle track that soon runs on between hedges to emerge on a lane close by a conspicuous radio mast.

Turn left and follow the lane down to the village of Sandwith. As you enter the village, turn left, walk past the **Dog and Partridge pub**, and continue along the lane to a T-junction at Lanehead Ⓑ. Cross the road and go into the lane opposite (signposted for St Bees road via Demesne). The lane soon becomes a narrow path between hedgerows.

When you reach Demesne, swing left into the farmyard, and then turn right onto a Coast-to-Coast footpath that runs between farm buildings and out along a broad track to reach the St Bees road. Cross the road and go down the lane opposite to Bell House and Woodside. After the buildings, the track descends to cross a cattle-grid. Shortly, when the track forks, keep right to reach a gate after which the track starts to descend. At a low waymark Ⓒ, the Coast-to-Coast takes its leave, descending left to a gate. Now simply keep on with the main track to pass Stanley Farm, and continue on a broad track.

Follow the ongoing track as far as a waymark where it turns left to go down to a railway crossing. Here leave the track and keep on in the same direction. The way is pathless, but follows the course of an old wall that will guide you to two stiles at the bottom corner of distant Abbey Wood.

Cross the stiles and continue at the top edge of a rough pasture, walking parallel with the woodland boundary. On the far side of the wood, pass through a makeshift sheep enclosure and press on along a broad track beyond. This runs on to a kissing-gate giving into a large car park adjoining St Bees School. Walk past the school buildings and out to meet a road. Turn left and walk down towards St Bees centre. Just on passing the priory church, turn right onto a signposted path that runs across fields towards the coast.

On the far side, the path makes two escapes from the field. On the right, steps lead up to a gate giving onto Abbey Road: turn left and in a few strides, bear right. The other runs on to emerge on another road: turn right. Both ways soon rejoin, and all that remains is to follow the road out to the beach and the conclusion of the walk. ●

Upper Eskdale and Great Moss

		GPS waypoints
Start	Brotherilkeld	🖉 NY 213 011
Distance	8 miles (12.5km)	Ⓐ NY 227 036
Height gain	1,345 feet (410m)	Ⓑ NY 217 052
Approximate time	4 hours	Ⓒ NY 214 024
Parking	At foot of Hardknott Pass (roadside)	
Route terrain	Rugged but generally on a clear path; river crossing	
Ordnance Survey maps	Landranger 90 (Penrith & Keswick), Explorer OL6 (The English Lakes – South-western area)	

The main thrust of Eskdale is, up to a point – that point being the end of the Ravenglass and Eskdale railway line at Boot – quite well known, but it is not over-populated even at the height of summer. This is a lush, green valley dominated by rocky outcrops that hint at more rugged ground not far distant. The whole area was once managed by the monks of Furness Abbey, and once (in pre-National Park days) threatened with almost complete afforestation. That ruggedness is close by, for from the foot of the Hardknott Pass, at Brotherilkeld below the Roman fort, the valley turns north-eastwards, dividing into two as it reaches the craggy circle of hills formed by Crinkle Crags, Bowfell, Esk Pike, Ill Crag and the two highest summits in England, Scafell Pike and Scafell; the rather more modest Slight Side completes the ring.

In its lower reaches, Eskdale was most likely the first of the Lakeland valleys to be accessed by the Norse people. Then as now, Upper Eskdale is largely uninhabited save for a scattering of farms and hundreds of sheep.

The walk into the huge amphitheatre, known as Great Moss, regularly sees the passage of walkers' boots, but as arenas in Lakeland go, this is less well known. Yet it is a fabulous place; ruggedly handsome, demanding and very isolated in poor weather, but incredibly

beautiful. Few people venture here for Great Moss alone; most may well be heading across Esk Hause to more distant valleys, or trudging up towards Mickledore – Samuel Taylor Coleridge's 'hyphen' between Scafell and its 'fierce yet irresistible neighbour' – for passage onto Scafell Pike (or Doe Crag as it was known in the days before tourists), or left to Foxes Tarn to bag Scafell. But the route described here combines green valleys, rough pathways, river scenery, waterfalls, that glorious atmospheric

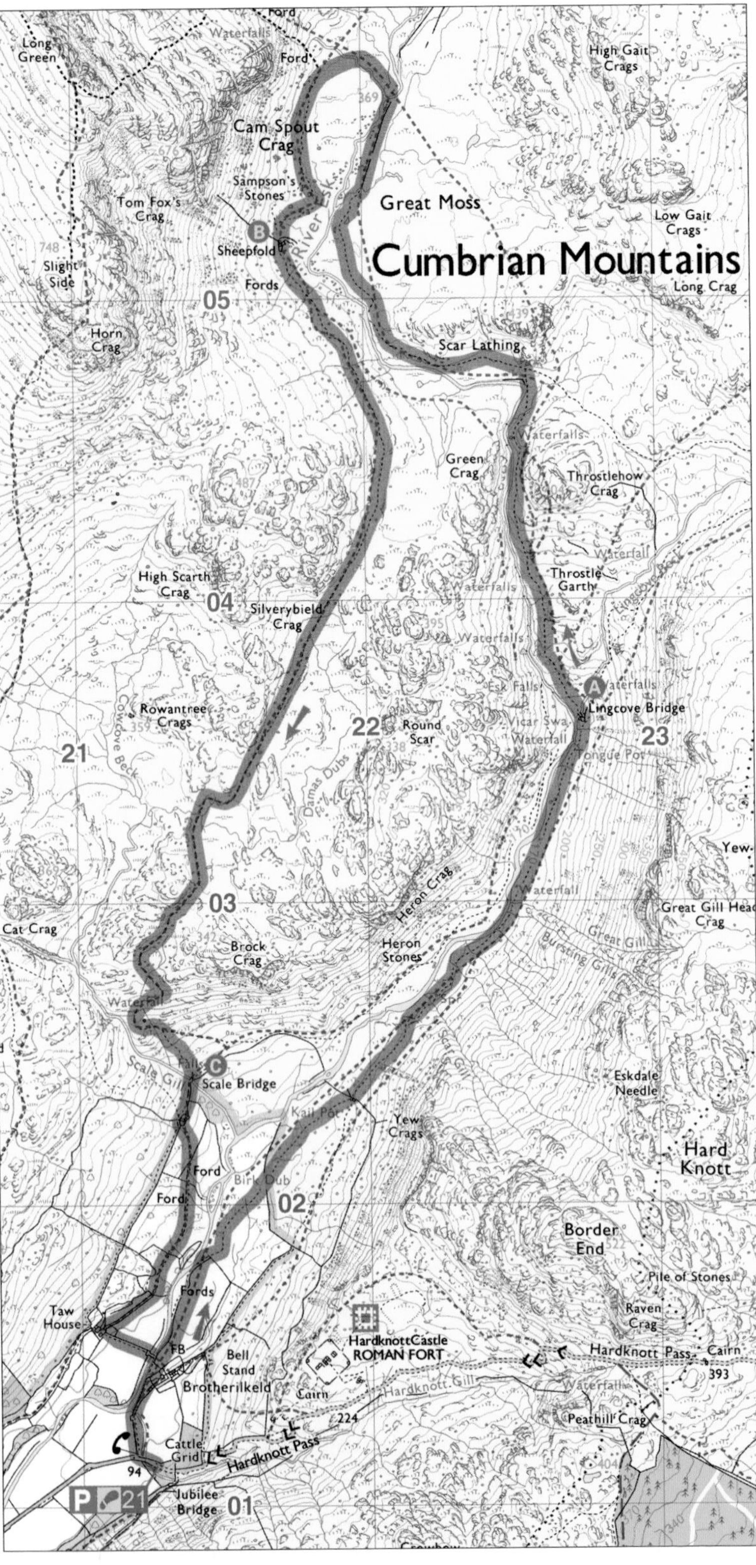

SCALE 1:25000 or 2½ INCHES to 1 MILE *4CM to 1KM*

Great Moss

bowl below England's highest peaks, and a fine return through a valley that is virtually unknown.

🔦 Begin from the roadside parking area just above the cattle-grid on the Hardknott side of the road at Brotherilkeld, and walk down the road. Immediately after a small hump-backed bridge, turn right passing a telephone box and go forward along an access track to Brotherilkeld Farm.

Just on reaching the farm, bear left on a footpath signposted to 'Upper Eskdale'. Immediately beyond a wooden kissing-gate, ignore a footbridge spanning the River Esk (you'll come back this way), and continue up-river along its true left bank. The ongoing path follows a clear route as it crosses rough pastures, moving steadily towards the dominant fells of Crinkle Crags and Bowfell at the head of the valley.

Gradually, the path climbs away from the river and leads up to a ladder-stile crossing the intake wall beyond which a stony path continues across brackeny slopes, before steadily descending, once more to parallel the river.

Continue up-river to handsome Lingcove Bridge Ⓐ where the River Esk has its confluence with Lingcove Beck. Cross the bridge and keep on, now on a rising stony track that ascends steeply above the Esk. Go on through a narrow gap between Throstlehow Crag and Green Crag, and a short way on follow a narrow path as it loops around to bypass a boggy section below Scar Lathing. The crossing point is not especially clear, but the path below Scar Lathing is, so cross to it as soon as you can do so dry-shod and follow the path, left, around the end of Scar Lathing, turning finally northwards to reach the southern edge of Great Moss.

Once on the expanse of Great Moss the crossing point for the river will always be determined by recent weather conditions, and it may be necessary to walk some way up the dale before a crossing can be made. Of course, if you

0	200	400	600	800 METRES	1
					KILOMETRES
					MILES
0	200	400	600 YARDS	½	

have spare socks and a towel with you, you can cross almost anywhere except in spate conditions. *If the river cannot be crossed safely, the only course is to retreat.* Wherever the river is crossed, bear left on the other side and follow a clear track below the rocky slopes of Scafell and Cam Spout Crag to a sheepfold **B**. A clear path leaves the sheepfold, ascending left across a grassy slope.

The path initially heads for Green Crag, but then, gaining height gently, swings round to a more southerly direction and continues as a clear stony path that pursues a delightful route through a hidden valley. It is never in doubt, but the path casts about a bit to avoid the worst of the wet ground. When it emerges at the other end, with the bulk of Harter Fell looming ahead, the path swings left to descend to the River Esk once more.

Towards the valley bottom, the route bears right to parallel the intake wall. Just after Scale Bridge **C**, the descending track branches. Take to the lower path, which soon leads to a gate giving into a sloping pasture. Go down this, the path rather indistinct, but roughly following the course of a stream (often dried up) and passing a large ash tree.

The route eventually runs into a walled track leading to Taw House, the ancestral home of a family of statesmen named Towers. It was to Taw House that Coleridge – the first Lakeland fell walker – made for following his epic descent of Scafell on 5 August 1802, and from whence the next day his host, John Vicar ('Vic') Towers, took him back up the valley to explore a few more crags before lunch.

At Taw House (now a National Trust property), cross a ladder-stile on the left and go down the left-hand edge of a pasture to a step-stile in a field corner giving onto a bridge spanning the River Esk (the bridge passed at the start of the walk). Over the bridge, turn right onto the outward route near Brotherilkeld Farm. Pass through a kissing-gate, and retrace the outward route. ●

River Esk on the way to Lingcove Bridge

Torver Commons and Walna Scar

		GPS waypoints	
Start	Coniston		
Distance	8¼ miles (13.2km)	🏁	SD 304 975
Height gain	1,425 feet (435m)	Ⓐ	SD 300 947
Approximate time	4 hours	Ⓑ	SD 285 945
		Ⓒ	SD 273 965
Parking	Coniston (Pay and Display)	Ⓓ	SD 289 970
Route terrain	Lakeshore paths; woodland; rugged moors and mosses; stony fell tracks	Ⓔ	SD 285 981
Ordnance Survey maps	Landranger 97 (Kendal & Morecambe), Explorer OL7 (The English Lakes – South-eastern area)		

The Torver Commons cover a wide area. The lakeside commons offer relaxed strolling before a complete contrast by climbing up to an ancient packhorse thoroughfare, the Walna Scar Road, that runs along the rugged base of the Coniston Fells. The walk concludes with a loop northwards to gaze down into Coppermines Valley.

🏁 Leave the centre of Coniston along the A593, and as you approach the edge of the village centre, turn left into Lake Road. As you reach the Lake Road Estate, where the road bends to the left, leave it by climbing over a stile on the right into a large pasture and onto a footpath for Torver via the Lakeshore. The path is level and offers fine views of the Coniston Fells, and glimpses of Coniston Water through lakeside trees. Pass through a gate and continue beside a fence towards a small wooded mound. When the fence ends, turn left following a wide track down towards the lakeshore.

As you approach the lakeshore the path bends towards a farm and camping site based around Coniston Hall. Pass to the right of Coniston Hall, and stay on a surfaced lane to pass an outbuilding and then continue on a clear lane. After passing through a gate you enter the grounds of a seasonal campsite. Follow the main surfaced track, drawing ever closer to the lake, and then at a waymark branching left onto a stony track that leads to a gate in a wall, beyond which you now follow the lakeshore.

Five miles long, and with a depth approaching 200 feet, Coniston Water is the third largest of the lakes. In 1967, Donald Campbell was killed on Coniston Water while attempting the water speed record, which he had originally broken in 1955. After a couple of gates you reach a signpost pointing a way to the right for Torver; ignore this, and keep on along the lakeshore towards Torver Common Wood. Shortly the path is deflected a little way inland to pass round a small copse, but soon enters Torver Commons, where you return to the lakeshore.

When you next reach a signpost for

Torver **Ⓐ**, turn right, leaving the lakeshore. The path climbs to leave the Torver Commons at a gate, beyond which it continues through more light woodland, with Dow Crag and the Old Man of Coniston once more in view. After passing through a couple of gates and some derelict buildings, the path becomes enclosed between a hedgebank and a moss-covered wall.

You pass Brackenbarrow Farm, and then walk out along a broader access track to intercept a narrow lane. Cross this and go over a step-stile opposite and then take to a muddy path across rough pasture to a kissing-gate, beyond which the path is less of a quagmire. After a short section of boardwalk, keep to the right-hand edge of a field to reach the A593.

Turn left and walk beside the road for about 100 yds, and then leave the main road at a bend **Ⓑ**, by turning right up a narrow lane to Scarr Head. Follow the lane, signposted for Tranearth and Walna Scar, turning right at Scarr Head Cottage onto a surfaced bridleway. When the surfacing ends a rough track takes over.

Eventually, at a barn, the track breaks free of constraining walls, and continues across rough moorland with outstanding views of the Coniston Fells. A concrete

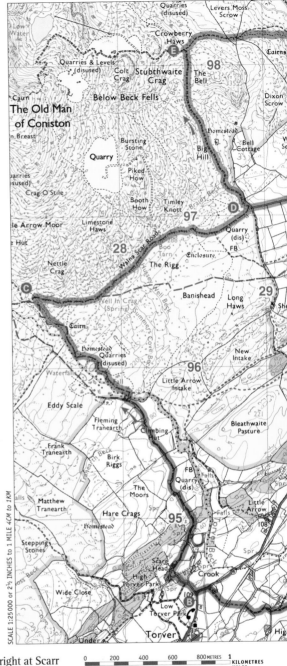

footbridge takes you over Tranearth Beck, beyond which the track continues towards an area of quarry spoil.

After three gates in quick succession, you cross Torver Beck. Stay with the

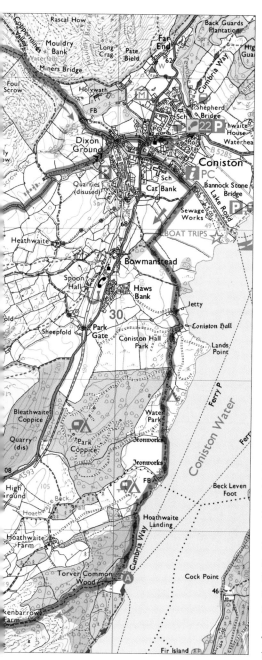

little importance, which is used. The road is a clear stony track running roughly east to west, and, if you stay approximately along the line of Torver Beck or any of the streams flowing down from Little Arrow Moor, you will intercept it. When you do, turn right, and follow it through twists and turns and narrow rock passages, and passing reed-filled Boo Tarn, until it ends at a gate beyond which lies a surfaced lane. Here you have the choice of taking the lane, which will provide you with a direct return to Coniston village.

But the walk continues by turning left Ⓓ along what is the most popular route onto the Old Man of Coniston. The track climbs steadily, passing the very shapely minor top called The Bell – you can make an easy diversion to include this superb vantage point if time permits, using a clear grassy path that branches right from the main stony track you are following.

Eventually, just after passing through a couple of rocky jaws, as the Old Man path circles to the left Ⓔ, you can leave it for a clear path descending on the right towards Coniston, and offering a fine view, as does The Bell, of Coppermines Valley.

track as it now bears to the left below slate spoil. Once above this, the track bears to the right to pass around the quarry itself, into which a fine waterfall plummets, filling a lake with no apparent outflow.

A number of tracks now lead up to the Walna Scar Road Ⓒ, and it is of

The path is straightforward and leads all the way down to the outskirts of Coniston. At Dixon Ground Farm, you reach a lanehead. Keep forward, and at the **Sun Hotel** turn left and walk down to the village centre, opposite the **Yewdale Hotel**, from where you retrace your steps to the car park.   ●

Scafell Pike and Scafell

Start	Wasdale	**GPS waypoints**	
Distance	5½ miles (9km)	🥾	NY 183 075
Height gain	3,610 feet (1,100m)	Ⓐ	NY 195 074
		Ⓑ	NY 211 077
Approximate time	4 hours	Ⓒ	NY 210 069
Parking	Near Brackenclose	Ⓓ	NY 207 065
Route terrain	Rugged mountain slopes; loose scree in places		
Ordnance Survey maps	Landrangers 89 (West Cumbria) and 90 (Penrith & Keswick), Explorer OL6 (The English Lakes – South-western area)		

In spite of the ascent from Wasdale being the shortest and least troublesome of the routes onto the Scafells, this combination with Scafell is never going to be a simple stroll, indeed it is very demanding and can be intimidating for less experienced walkers at the best of times. *But as an exercise in walk planning the format of the route cannot be bettered.*
The major difficulties are associated with Scafell and not Scafell Pike, leaving those with no appetite for crag-related exploration to call it a day on reaching the highest summit in England; Scafell will always wait another day, and does have less complex albeit longer approaches.

🥾 From the car park near the campsite, head for the bridge that spans Lingmell Gill and turn left, following the stream, keeping Brackenclose, a climbers' club hut, on your right. Cross a footbridge and keep along the line of the gill. Beyond a fence, ignore a path going left on to the shoulder of Lingmell (though strong walkers could rewardingly add this fell to the day's walk, and rejoin this route at Lingmell col).

Continue climbing with the gill until, after a wall, you need to cross it once more to gain Brown Tongue Ⓐ, framed by streams and directly below Hollow Stones and Mickledore. As you reach the edge of Hollow Stones go left along

a cairned path to Lingmell Col **B**, from where a stony path leads upwards, directly to the summit of Scafell Pike; rock all the way.

From Scafell Pike take the rocky path down to Mickledore **C**. *This is the point at which some may decide, not unreasonably, to abandon Scafell, and to opt for a descent from Mickledore in a north-westerly direction, down through the spectacular arena of Hollow Stones, to rejoin the upward route on Brown Tongue; rough going in its early stages.*

There is an interesting tale about Hollow Stones. Rock climbers have been exploring the cliffs of the Scafells for generations, and one of them had an unsettling experience here during the First World War. His closest friend, and keen rock climber, had gone to fight in France. One sunny summer afternoon, the man descending Hollow Stones, was unexpectedly caught up by his old friend. They walked down the fell together, yarning of the past and the days they would share on the crags once the war was ended. Down in the valley, the soldier announced that he had to continue to another valley,

Scafell from Scafell Pike

promising he would see the other soon. For days the man thought about his old friend, and then arrived a letter from France: the friend had been killed in action on the very afternoon he believed he had walked with him down to Wasdale Head.

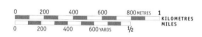

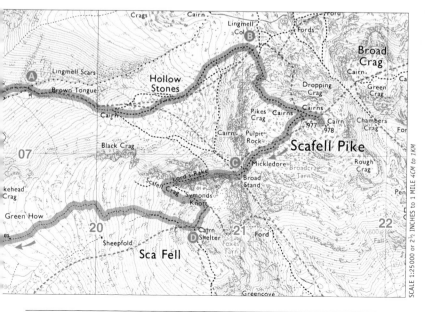

On the summit of Scafell Pike

So, set off up Lord's Rake, and scramble awkwardly to the first obvious col, a narrow transverse ledge, barely wide enough to stand on. A short descent and re-ascent takes you to a second col from which the third can be seen ahead. To reach it, another descent on a rough path precedes more of the same as you climb out of the rake.

As you leave the rake, turn left to ascend a rocky path to a small plateau with a minor top, Symonds Knott, on your left. A branching path, heading right, soon leads you to the massively cairned summit of Scafell . This is a precious and to-be-treasured moment for so few of those who achieve the summit of Scafell Pike bother to take on its sibling, yet it really is a worthy companion.

After so much rock work it will come as a surprise that the way back to Wasdale – unless you are keen to revisit Lord's Rake in descent – lies down sweeping grassy flanks, roughly west, over Green How to meet an old corpse road north of Fence Wood. Turn right here to descend to Brackenclose, where your outward route is rejoined.

As an alternative, as you leave Scafell summit, by treading a little more to the south from Green How, you can reach Burnmoor Tarn, a splendid location, and from there join the corpse road heading north; if anything the gradient is a little easier, but it adds distance. ●

If not descending to Hollow Stones, cross Mickledore to make a daunting and intimate acquaintance with Scafell Crag, and then descend a badly eroded path on the right that keeps close to the base of the crag. *This is an intimidating place on the best of days,* and takes you to the foot of a feature known as Lord's Rake, a slanting and undulating route across the cliff face, for many years, after thousands of boots, a rather bare and daring gully rising between the crags of Scafell and a subsidiary buttress on the right. At the start of the rake, a cross, carved in the rock commemorates the death in 1903 of four pioneer rock climbers who fell from the crags above this spot. *No amount of footpath reparation is going to make Lord's Rake a walk in the park, and care is needed every step of the way.*

Dow Crag and Goat's Water

		GPS waypoints	
Start	Torver		
Distance	7 miles (11.5km)	🏁 SD 285 945	
Height gain	2,395 feet (730m)	Ⓐ SD 273 965	
Approximate time	4 hours	Ⓑ SD 258 965	
Parking	Lay-by on the A593, near lane junction	Ⓒ SD 266 983	
Route terrain	Rugged mountain tops and tracks; *not advised in poor visibility*		
Ordnance Survey maps	Landranger 96 (Barrow-in-Furness & South Lakeland), Explorer OL6 (The English Lakes – South-western area)		

This is a pleasant but challenging walk making use of old quarry tracks to gain height to the top of Walna Scar, a high mountain pass linking Coniston with Dunnerdale. The way continues along a fine rocky ridge to the top of Dow Crag overlooking Goat's Water, by way of which the walk concludes, although you can quite easily reverse the loop around Goat's Water and the Dow Crag ridge once you reach the Walna Scar Road – there is a good track/path all the way.

The moors above Torver have been settled since prehistoric times. W. G. Collingwood, in *The Lake Counties* writes, 'All these fells must once have been the happy hunting-grounds of primitive races, children of the mist, perhaps surviving long after the outskirts were settled by civilized folk.' Originally a Norse settlement, Torver received its name from the Norse word for turf. A path led through the hamlet from Furness Abbey and was used by the monks. Torver was also a staging post for a packhorse trail over the Walna Scar pass to the Duddon Valley.

Long involved with the many traditional industries of Lakeland – stone and slate quarrying, iron smelting, charcoal production, bobbin manufacture, farming and milling – Torver, overlooking Coniston Water,

developed significantly when the Furness Railway came here in 1859. Farming was also an early enterprise around Torver, and there was a time when the Herdwick sheep far outnumbered people.

Although a 12th-century chapel stood on the site of the present-day church of St Luke, burials were not permitted there until 1538; before then the village's dead had to be carried to Ulverston. When Archbishop Cranmer authorised burials at Torver, the long, bier-laden treks over mountain passes ended. A new church was built in 1849, and that replaced by St Luke's in 1883-4. The nearby Church House Inn as a building dates from the 14th century, but doesn't appear in the records as an inn until 1851, when it is listed as Kirk House Inn.

Leave the lay-by by heading along the branching tarmac lane signposted to Coniston Old Man and Walna Scar. Follow the waymarking through the hamlet of Scarr Head, and at Scarr Head Cottage turn right to join a walled bridleway. Walk on until you reach a bridge spanning Tranearth Beck, then continue by a rough track to gated sheep pens. Waymarking now directs you to a bridge over Torver Beck. Once across the bridge turn left to pass along the base of quarry waste heaps, before climbing beside a tree-lined gully – *the entrance to quarry workings, and dangerous.*

Climb to a fence, turn right to circle the edge of the quarry, and on the opposite side take a terraced path left, climbing to the Walna Scar Road **A**. Turn left to cross a packhorse bridge over Torver Beck. Once across the bridge the track becomes more eroded as it climbs to a large cairn. Continue, ascending all the while, passing small cairns and a small stone shelter on the right.

A small cairn marks the top of the Walna Scar Road, a high mountain pass **B** from where there is a fine view down into Dunnerdale. Turn right and ascend

Dow Crag and Buck Pike from Walna Scar

a grassy path to a stone shelter on the top of Brown Pike, the first of two fell tops en route to Dow Crag. From here on, the views are consistently impressive, and the high-level walking of supreme quality.

From the shelter the path heads north along the rim of the corrie that houses

approach Dow Crag, the immense cliffs falling to Goat's Water below become more pronounced and the path crosses the top of one or two yawning gullies; *children will need close supervision here, and while on the fine rocky summit of Dow Crag.*

From this point everything is downhill, but only physically. You may be leaving behind the magnificent views from the top of Dow Crag, but the return beside Goat's Water is walking of the highest order.

From the top of Dow Crag go north, continuing your original direction, on a clear rocky path which soon turns north-east to descend to Goat's Hawse **ⓒ**, a boggy col linking Dow Crag and the Old Man of Coniston.

Go down to the Hawse and as the path starts to ascend on the other side take a path off to the right and descend to Goat's Water. *The path is loose and slippery in places.*

Use the path along the left shore of Goat's Water, passing through scattered boulders, and following a good path that leads all the way out of the valley, to a cairn on the Walna Scar Road, not far from the point at which you first joined it.

Cross the track to a green path, and descend to the wire fencing around Bannishead Quarry, from where you retrace your steps to Torver. ●

Blind Tarn. Press on along the ridge, crossing another minor summit, Buck Pike, on the way, and then heading for Dow Crag by a stony path. As you

Black Combe

		GPS waypoints
Start	Whicham	SD 135 826
Distance	8½ miles (13.5km). Shorter version 5 miles (8km)	Ⓐ SD 131 828
Height gain	2,185 feet (666m). Shorter version 1,853 feet (565m)	Ⓑ SD 134 853 Ⓒ SD 117 870
Approximate time	4½ hours. Shorter version 3 hours	Ⓓ SD 125 828
Parking	Lay-by on the A595, near Whicham church, or, on days when there is no church service, there is a larger parking area adjacent to the church	
Route terrain	Rugged fell tops and tracks; *not advised in poor visibility*	
Ordnance Survey maps	Landranger 96 (Barrow-in-Furness & South Lakeland), Explorer OL6 (The English Lakes – South-western area)	

The beauty of Black Combe is not its face, which is rather plain, but its unrivalled views, unimpeded by intervening hills or woodlands. This is a scintillating, connoisseur's fell, achieved by a clean and simple line that is never in doubt. The fell does not quite achieve the notoriety that a height of 2,000 ft brings, but it just tops 600m, which, for want of a better excuse, is reason enough to visit this isolated top.
Many walkers want simply to return from the summit – although there are actually two summits, one with a massive cairn – and that is a fine enough excursion. But this walk offers a much longer expedition that wanders off into the voluptuous embrace of the north-western fell slopes.

Walk to the church, and go past it into a narrow pathway that emerges onto a very narrow lane leading up to Kirkbank. Turn left at the lane, and walk up to the farm. Keep to the right of the buildings and walk into an enclosed track that runs around the farm boundary to reach open fell Ⓐ. Here the track forks. Turn right and walk up to a gate/stile. After that, the way is never in doubt and climbs incessantly upwards. There is a brief steeper section quite early on, but after that the ascent is gradual. However, the wide path you

are following does not take you to the summit. To reach that, you must leave the path at a bend Ⓑ, and walk up an easy slope to the trig pillar surrounded by a stone shelter and with the most breathtaking view into the heart of the Lakeland fells.

To the south, beyond an intervening tarn, there lies a slightly lower summit, but one that has a massive cairn. From this hoary fell top in distant wardening

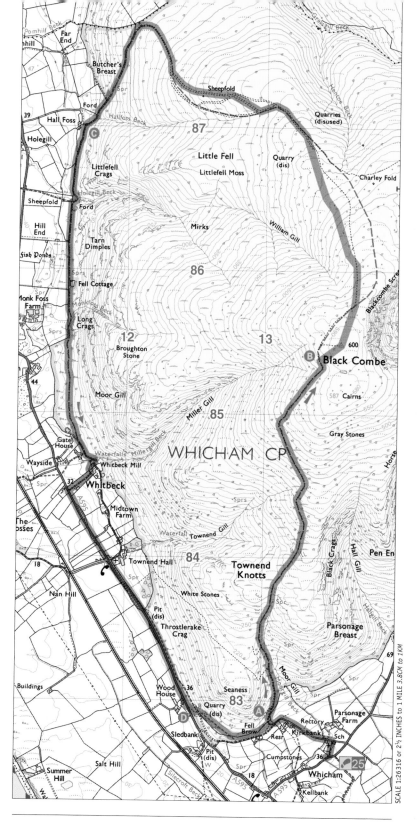

Whicham church

days, the author accomplished the 'Most Unusual Mountain Rescue of the Year' by carrying back to Whicham tucked inside his anorak what at first glance had been just another iced rock in the enormous cairn. In reality it was a sad and sorrowful cat that had somehow found its way onto the fell top, and would surely have died had he not chanced along and shared his coffee with it. On reaching Kirkbank, the cat skittered away into the farm buildings.

From the top of Black Combe you can simply retreat the way you came, and many do. *But to tackle the longer walk, leave the summit by heading northwards.* An indistinct path starts from the trig, but then improves, becoming a quad bike track. Take care not to descend too far to the right (east), as there is a similar path heading down Black Combe ridge. Once on the correct track – it runs roughly north-westwards, but not quite as the line marked on the map until much lower down – it is simply a question of following its easy and untroubled course until it finally descends almost to a wall, where it intercepts another track overlooking Bootle, with Barfield Tarn clearly in view to the left.

Turn left and walk beside a fence. An earlier shortcut from the higher track brings you down to the fence also.

Continue alongside the fence, and then a wall and descend towards the ruins of Hall Foss Farm **C**. Here turn left to discover that the path is now a delightful green track beside the wall, one that leads on to cross deeply incised Holegill Beck, which may require a bit of nifty boulder hopping to cross dry-shod.

Resume the wallside track, which leads up past derelict Fell Cottage before pressing on to cross the base of Monkfoss Beck, which displays a couple of neat waterfalls. When the track, which is now a green swathe through bracken, forks (SD 115 854), keep left, sticking to the higher ground.

Eventually the track comes down to run beside a wall above the farms at Whitbeck. Here, keep alongside the wall and pass above the farms to reach Whitbeck Mill below the waterfalls of Millergill Beck. Follow a rough lane past cottages and farms, which after a cattle-grid becomes a pronounced vehicle track. The lane runs out to meet the A595. Turn left and walk beside the road, using verges as much as possible, and always taking care against approaching traffic. This short bout of unpleasantness is the price you pay for the pleasure of what has gone before. The roadside public footpath shown on maps does not exist on the ground; *so great care is needed here as you follow the road for almost one mile.*

At **D**, leave the road by climbing a steep bank on the left, and soon bearing right to cross a fell shoulder. The path eventually descends to run alongside a wall, and shortly a vehicle access. Keep forward along this, and soon you will meet the outward route. Walk down the lane and take the narrow path past the church to complete the walk.

Ennerdale

		GPS waypoints	
Start	Ennerdale Bridge		NY 085 154
Distance	11½ miles (18.5km)	Ⓐ	NY 131 138
Height gain	835 feet (255m)	Ⓑ	NY 165 135
Approximate time	5 hours	Ⓒ	NY 112 151
Parking	Two car parks at Broadmoor	Ⓓ	NY 090 158
Route terrain	Lakeside paths; forest trails		
Ordnance Survey maps	Landranger 89 (West Cumbria), Explorer OL4 (The English Lakes – North-western area)		

In spite of a long-standing reputation as a depressing place, 'claustrophobically blanketed' in dark pines, the long valley of Ennerdale is at last beginning to see the light. The cloak of trees, for so long the object of criticism, has been thinned and cleared. Walks have been introduced through and around the valley that appeal to walkers of all standards, and, still in the early stages of its eastbound journey, the Northern Coast-to-Coast Walk, renowned for its discerning quality, passes down the length of the valley before crossing to Honister Pass and Borrowdale. At the head of the dale, Pillar dominates, with Steeple close by, always peering across the expanse of the lake, or as mountain cameos through gaps in the trees. But best of all, there is no unauthorised vehicular access beyond Bowness Knott, the dale is the preserve of pedestrians only, and all the better for it.

This walk is in two parts, which may be dealt with separately if preferred. As a complete walk it is long, though never physically arduous, and is best reserved for a long summer's day. The first part circles Ennerdale Water; the second visits the forests at the head of the valley, returning easily along a broad woodland track.

Ennerdale lake

The walk begins from a car park near the western end of the lake, and about a mile east of Ennerdale Bridge. Go left after the car park, and follow a broad track to the foot of Ennerdale

Water. Here, turn right along the southern shore of the lake. Arrival at the edge of this substantial lake, across which the swelling sides of Great Borne and Starling Dodd soar bulkily upwards, is an inspiring moment.

Things have changed in Ennerdale Bridge since one traveller described the **pub** as 'small, dirty, and filled with roaring tipplers' – and that at nine in the morning! The village now sees few visitors, its general inaccessibility ensuring that the throngs do not stumble upon it other than inadvertently. Thankfully, it remains a quiet farming and forestry retreat, well known and loved by local people, but never likely to figure highly on tourist itineraries.

In prehistoric times, iron was smelted here, and much later haematite was mined along the valley of Ennerdale. There were also a number of small industries here related to weaving, and Ennerdale Bridge grew as a result.

A good path skirts the lake's shore, never far from the water until it encounters the rocky thrust of Angler's Crag. Strong walkers can leave the path a little before Angler's Crag and clamber over its summit for a splendid view of the valley, and a long steady descent to rejoin the lower path.

There is no denying the beauty of

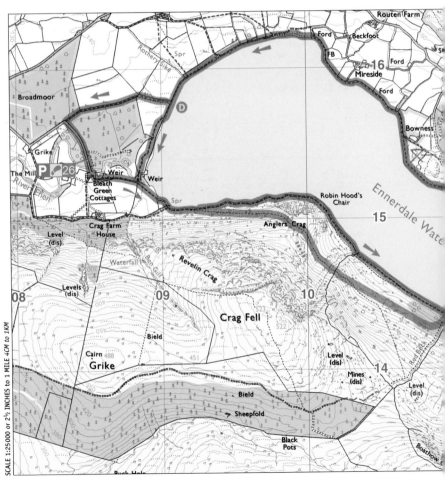

SCALE 1:25000 or 2½ INCHES to 1 MILE 4CM to 1KM

Ennerdale. Edwin Waugh, a notable Lancashire poet, and at his best when revelling in the wild and stormy side of nature, wrote a most evocative description of the lake in his *Rambles in the Lake Country*. Of a moonlit visit he penned: 'In this sheltered corner little eddies of shimmering silver flit about – the dainty Ariels of moonlit water; there, is a burnished islet of stirless brilliance, in which even the moon smiles to see herself look so passing fair; and, out beyond, the wide waters are in a tremulous fever of delight with her sweet influence ... If there be magic in the world, it is this!'

A less demanding option continues at a lower level, through the fractured base of the crag. Close by, a small headland jutting into the lake, is known as Robin Hood's Chair, though there is scant evidence that this legendary hero ever ventured this far. Even so, it's a significant moment for Coast-to-Coasters, as they're all heading for Robin Hood's Bay.

Once beyond Angler's Crag, the path continues pleasantly to the head of the lake, where a path Ⓐ sweeps round to join the main valley trail at Irish Bridge. By this route you can shorten the day, and return along the northern shore of the lake.

When the path starts heading for Irish Bridge, however, keep ahead to meet a forest trail that runs on across Woundell Beck and above the River Liza into Ling Mell Plantation. A number of walks have been constructed through the Ennerdale plantations, and the Liza Path is one of them, developed in 1985.

You now have a choice of routes. Either follow the main forest trail (by far the easier option), or pursue the Liza Path as it leaves the trail for a path at the forest edge. Pass Moss Dub, a small, overgrown tarn, before continuing roughly parallel with the river.

MAP CONTINUES ON PAGE 84 →

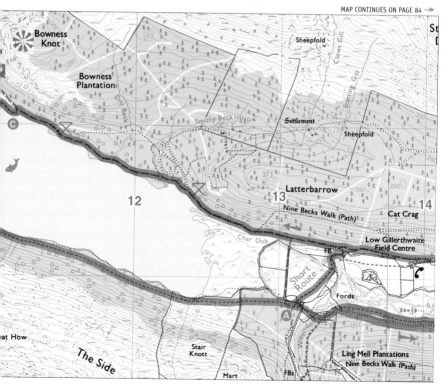

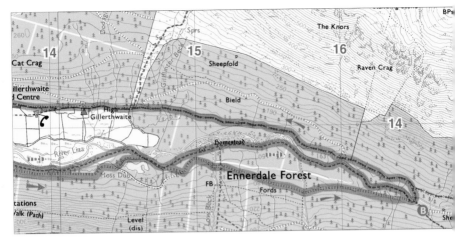

Along the way you pass an area of ancient settlements, probably Bronze Age, marked as a 'Homestead' on the map, before the path reaches Low Beck. The area around Gillerthwaite was the site of one of only a few vaccary homesteads in western Lakeland.

High Beck needs to be crossed, by a footbridge, and in due course the shoreline path rises to meet the forest trail near a bridge over the River Liza **B**.

Across the river, the main valley trail is soon reached. It goes right, through continuing forest to reach the

Ennerdale and Pillar

splendidly set Black Sail Youth Hostel, but your way lies left, following the broad trail towards the Bowness Knott car park.

Before reaching the car park, a path **C** leaves the main trail to go down to the lake shore, which is now followed closely around the northern loop of the lake to a point **D** where a path runs westwards to the Broadmoor woodland car park and the conclusion of the walk. *If you started at the car park just south of the Ehen Bridge, you can stay on the shore path a little longer to cross near the lake outflow after which you turn right to return to the car park.*

Pillar and Red Pike

Start	Wasdale	**GPS waypoints**	
Distance	10 miles (16km)	🖊 NY 168 068	
Height gain	4,235 feet (1,290m)	Ⓐ NY 187 090	
Approximate time	6 hours	Ⓑ NY 191 114	
Parking	Overbeck Bridge	Ⓒ NY 159 114	
Route terrain	Rugged mountain paths; *long and sometimes steep ascents and descents*	Ⓓ NY 174 096	
Ordnance Survey maps	Landranger 89 (West Cumbria), Explorers OL4 (The English Lakes – North-western area) and OL6 (The English Lakes – South-western area)		

The advantage of starting at Overbeck is that you get a generous warm up along the road (2 miles/3km) before you hit the rough ground of Mosedale. Strong walkers could make an extended embrace of Mosedale, following the valley's watershed throughout, by starting with a direct ascent of Kirk Fell. Without Kirk Fell, as here described, the walk is still demanding, but it will give one of the most memorable day's fell wandering.

🖊 Once you reach the **Wasdale Head Inn** you set off for Black Sail Pass, taking a signed route Ⓐ up the eastern side of Mosedale. The route is not especially difficult, but does start to climb more earnestly as you start up Gatherstone Beck.

On arriving at Black Sail Pass Ⓑ, after pausing to take in the view, set off north-westwards onto Looking Stead, a minor summit with a grandstand view over the northern face of Pillar and the conifer-cloaked flanks of Ennerdale. The ongoing path to Pillar rises in a series of grassy and rocky steps, a fine line with striking views. The top of Pillar is rather bald, the highest point identified by a trig point and shelter cairn. From near the northern edge of the summit plateau there is a sensational view down to Pillar Rock.

An easy descent leads across Wind Gap to climb the bouldery unnamed summit at the top of Black Crag. Press on above Mirk Cove and follow a wall to the top of Scoat Fell Ⓒ. This elongated fell is divided into Little Scoat Fell (reached first, and higher) and Great Scoat Fell, which is not visited on this walk. Between the two a spur branches off to descend quickly to a col linking Steeple. Although the distance and height gain is not included in the calculation, Steeple is too good to miss, and the modest expenditure of energy required to include it is unlikely to evoke distress. If you have the time, do it.

A good path leads south-east from Little Scoat Fell onto Red Pike, and from there continues in splendid style to Dore Head Ⓓ, immediately below Stirrup Crag on the northern flank of Yewbarrow. From Dore Head you can

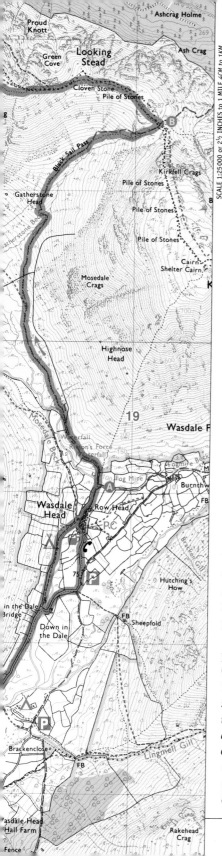

SCALE 1:25 000 or 2½ INCHES to 1 MILE 4CM to 1KM

Red Pike

truncate the walk by descending directly into Mosedale, keeping on grass to the left of a badly eroded spill of scree. *This descent is steep and with a sense of exposure, and likely to be troublesome in winter conditions or after rain.*

To complete the walk, you need to attack the grim face of Stirrup Crag, through which, perhaps surprisingly, an entertaining way is readily found. *Walkers with no taste for such craggy confrontation, however, need only move right, towards Over Beck, to find a steep grassy slope offering an easier, slanting line onto Yewbarrow.*

Continue across the airy top of Yewbarrow, a fabulous striding summit with super views, although in late July and August a diversion to the bilberry-laden slopes overlooking Wasdale could prove tasty.

As the ridge starts to drop, a good path leads you down through Dropping Crag and Bell Rib to Overbeck Bridge. *This descent requires care and can be slippery in almost all conditions. A winter descent is likely to prove awkward, and may require the use of crampons.*   ●

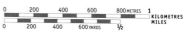

The Four Passes

		GPS waypoints	
Start	Wasdale Head		
Distance	15 miles (24km); 1½ miles (2.5km) less via Haystacks	🖉	NY 187 085
		Ⓐ	NY 192 114
Height gain	(full circuit) 4,430 feet (1,350m); (via Haystacks) 3,625 feet (1,105m)	Ⓑ	NY 189 133
		Ⓒ	NY 225 136
		Ⓓ	NY 235 122
Approximate time	(full circuit) 8 hours; (via Haystacks) 7 hours	Ⓔ	NY 235 109
		Ⓕ	NY 222 099
Parking	Wasdale		
Route terrain	Rugged mountain tracks; some road walking		
Ordnance Survey maps	Landranger 90 (Penrith and Keswick), Explorers OL4 (The English Lakes – North-western area) and OL6 (The English Lakes – South-western area)		

Suitable even for days when the tops are draped in mist, the Four Passes walk is an utterly refreshing circuit that slips neatly into any serious walker's portfolio; it is, however, a significant undertaking, suitable only for strong walkers. *Its basic construction is simple: you link the valleys of Wasdale, Ennerdale, Buttermere and Borrowdale by crossing four passes: Black Sails, Scarth Gap, Honister and Sty Head. Being circular, and touching base in each valley, you can plug into the circuit anywhere.*

Mosedale awaits, and at its head, the great bulk of Pillar, an inevitable attraction for anyone based in Wasdale and Ennerdale. Both these valleys have long been popular with walkers, though their relative inaccessibility tends to keep out the idly curious.

🖉 At Wasdale Head, go past the inn and onto the track that leads into Mosedale, trekking round the base of Kirk Fell, before rising a little more sternly by Gatherstone Beck to Black Sail Pass Ⓐ. From this mountain pass there is an undulating trod crossing from just below Black Sail Pass to Beck Head, between Great Gable and Kirk Fell (East top), and from there following Moses' Trod to Honister. Moses is said

to have been an illicit whisky distiller, working furtively on the slopes of Fleetwith Pike; more likely he was helping himself to plumbago, which in those days brought a good price, especially on the black market.

Onward the route descends sharply to the head of Ennerdale, arriving without complication at Black Sail Youth Hostel, one of the most imaginatively sited youth hostels in England, and an ideal base for anyone wanting to tackle this walk or the ascent of surrounding peaks over a few days.

Traffic is prohibited in Ennerdale, and results in the preservation here of a wild and rugged landscape. The once serried ranks of conifer that flanked the valley have seen some realignment, felling and replanting in recent years that has eased much of Ennerdale Forest's former rigidity, making it an altogether better place to wander.

Beyond the youth hostel, the walk keeps to the northern edge of the forest, rising easily to Scarth Gap **B**, with the great scree slope of Gamlin End rising to High Crag on the one hand, and less demanding Haystacks on the other. From here a path descending to Gatesgarth Farm at the head of the Buttermere Valley is pursued, there heading east, up the B5289 for the top of Honister **C**. Such, at least, is the conventional route, but walking up a road pass is unlikely to appeal to many when a vastly superior alternative is to hand.

(From Scarth Gap a variant route – linking **B** *and* **C** *– heads up the rock shoulder of Haystacks, and from there out across the great plateau of knolls and hollows between Haystacks and Honister. Innominate Tarn is first reached, a place of some poignancy for walkers reared on the Lakeland gospels according to the late Alfred Wainwright. Blackbeck Tarn, a little farther on has rather less appeal, though Nature's architecture here perfectly frames a picture of Buttermere beyond Warnscale Bottom. On crossing Black Beck a path ascends to the remains of Dubs Quarry, where a few ruinous buildings mark the start of a long gradual climb to a point overlooking the slate quarry at Honister.)*

A short way down the road from Honister Hause a track branches left. This was the original line down to Borrowdale, and a toll road that now sees a steady flow of pedestrian traffic. As Seatoller is reached, the old road swings round to meet the new road at a gate.

Now walk down to the branching road from Seatoller to Seathwaite Farm **D**. Beyond the farm buildings, a broad path escorts the combined forces of

Styhead Gill and Grains Gill, here the River Derwent, as far as the old packhorse bridge, Stockley Bridge **E**. Through a gate, ignoring a track going left beside a wall, a path ahead injects a little ascent, pulling up towards a small plantation that conceals the white mare's tail of Taylorgill Force. Climbing steadily, a rough track presses on to a wooden bridge spanning Styhead Gill, beyond which Styhead Tarn **F** reposes in a vast hollow flanked by some of the highest of Lakeland's mountains – Great Gable, Lingmell, Scafell Pike, Broad Crag, Great End.

(Between Seathwaite and the wooden bridge spanning Styhead Gill, a variant route, with a better view of Taylorgill Force, is available. This leaves Seathwaite by an archway through barns, as if heading for Sour Milk Gill and the hanging valley of Gillercombe. Once the Derwent, is crossed, however, a path, initially muddy, skirts the bottom of a small copse, roughly parallel with the Stockley Bridge path. Gradually, this climbs and later turns the corner of Base Brown and scampers to a gate in a most curious spot. A little nimble footwork on easy rising rocks soon leads on towards Taylorgill Force, followed by a steady rise, keeping close by Styhead Gill, to the wooden bridge and, before long, Sty Head Pass.)

Sty Head is unquestionably one of the finest spots in Lakeland, and a popular crossroads as walkers launch themselves in all directions. Not surprisingly a number of tracks radiate from Sty Head, and a little caution is needed to get the right one, heading down towards Wasdale, high above Lingmell Beck.

The valley bottom is reached near Burnthwaite Farm, one of only a few farms remaining active in Wasdale. From here it is just a short way to complete the walk.

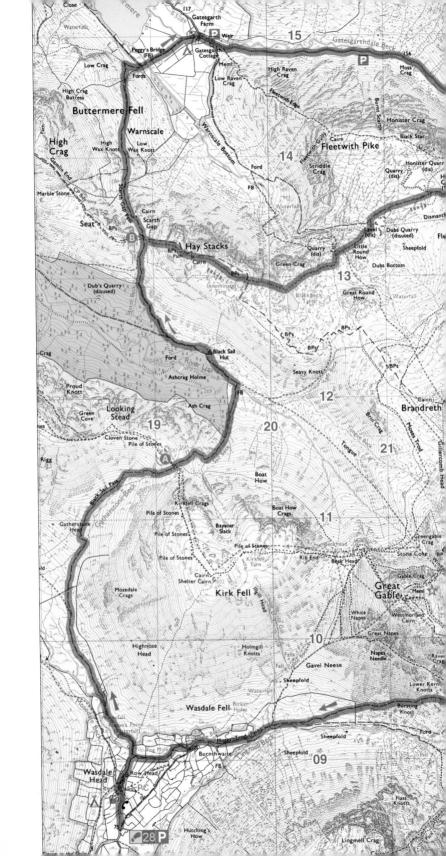

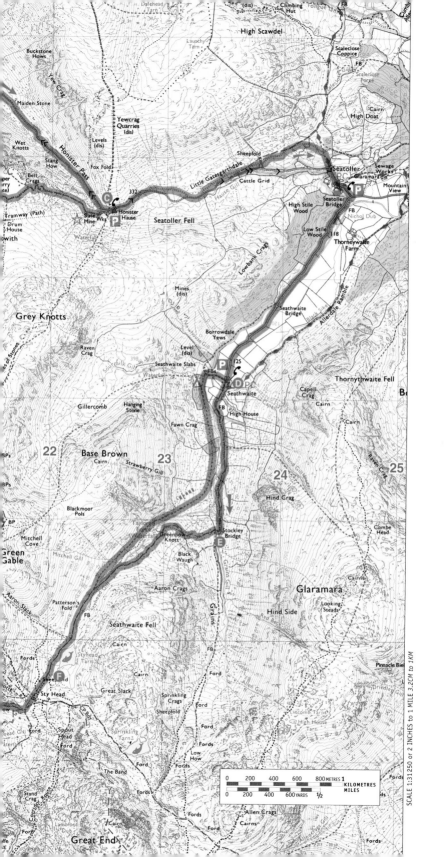

SCALE 1:31250 or 2 INCHES to 1 MILE 3.2CM to 1KM

Further Information

 ### Safety on the Hills

The hills, mountains and moorlands of Britain, though of modest height compared with those in many other countries, need to be treated with respect. Friendly and inviting in good weather, they can quickly be transformed into wet, misty, windswept and potentially dangerous areas of wilderness in bad weather. Even on an outwardly fine and settled summer day, conditions can rapidly deteriorate at high altitudes and, in winter, even more so.

Therefore it is advisable to always take both warm and waterproof clothing, sufficient nourishing food, a hot drink, first-aid kit, torch and whistle. Wear suitable footwear, such as strong walking-boots or shoes that give a good grip over rocky terrain and on slippery slopes. Try to obtain a local weather forecast and bear it in mind before you start. Do not be afraid to abandon your proposed route and return to your starting point in the event of a sudden and unexpected deterioration in the weather. Do not go alone and allow enough time to finish the walk well before nightfall.

Most of the walks described in this book do not venture into remote wilderness areas and will be safe to do, given due care and respect, at any time of year in all but the most unreasonable weather. Indeed, a crisp, fine winter day often provides perfect walking conditions, with firm ground underfoot and a clarity that is not possible to achieve in the other seasons of the year. A few walks, however, are suitable only for reasonably fit and experienced hill walkers able to use a compass and should definitely not be tackled by anyone else during the winter months or in bad weather, especially high winds and mist. These are indicated in the general description that precedes each of the walks.

 ### Walkers and the Law

The Countryside and Rights of Way Act (CRoW Act 2000) extends the rights of access previously enjoyed by walkers in England and Wales. Implementation of these rights began on 19 September 2004. The Act amends existing legislation and for the first time provides access on foot to certain types of land – defined as mountain, moor, heath, down and registered common land.

Where You Can Go
Rights of Way
Prior to the introduction of the CRoW Act, walkers could only legally access the countryside along public rights of way. These are either 'footpaths' (for walkers only) or 'bridleways' (for walkers, riders on horseback and pedal cyclists). A third category called 'Byways open to all traffic' (BOATs), is used by motorised vehicles as well as those using non-mechanised transport. Mainly they are green lanes, farm and estate roads, although occasionally they will be found crossing mountainous area.

Rights of way are marked on Ordnance Survey maps. Look for the green broken lines on the Explorer maps, or the red dashed lines on Landranger maps.

The term 'right of way' means exactly what it says. It gives a right of passage over what, for the most part, is private land. Under pre-CRoW legislation walkers were required to keep to the line of the right of way and not stray onto land on either side. If you did inadvertently wander off the right of way, either because of faulty map reading or because the route was not clearly indicated on the ground, you were technically trespassing.

Local authorities have a legal obligation to ensure that rights of way are kept clear and free of obstruction, and are signposted where they leave metalled roads. The duty of local authorities to install signposts extends to the placing of signs along a path or way, but only where the authority considers it necessary to have a signpost or waymark to assist persons unfamiliar with the locality.

Countryside Access Charter

Your rights of way are:

- public footpaths – on foot only. Sometimes waymarked in yellow
- bridleways – on foot, horseback and pedal cycle. Sometimes waymarked in blue
- byways (usually old roads), most 'roads used as public paths' and, of course, public roads – all traffic has the right of way

Use maps, signs and waymarks to check rights of way. Ordnance Survey Explorer and Landranger maps show most public rights of way

On rights of way you can:

- take a pram, pushchair or wheelchair if practicable
- take a dog (on a lead or under close control)
- take a short route round an illegal obstruction or remove it sufficiently to get past

You have a right to go for recreation to:

- public parks and open spaces – on foot
- most commons near older towns and cities – on foot and sometimes on horseback
- private land where the owner has a formal agreement with the local authority

In addition you can use the following by local or established custom or consent, but ask for advice if you are unsure:

- many areas of open country, such as moorland, fell and coastal areas, especially those in the care of the National Trust, and some commons
- some woods and forests, especially those owned by the Forestry Commission
- country parks and picnic sites
- most beaches
- canal towpaths
- some private paths and tracks Consent sometimes extends to horse-riding and cycling

For your information:

- county councils and London boroughs maintain and record rights of way, and register commons
- obstructions, dangerous animals, harassment and misleading signs on rights of way are illegal and you should report them to the county council
- paths across fields can be ploughed, but must normally be reinstated within two weeks
- landowners can require you to leave land to which you have no right of access
- motor vehicles are normally permitted only on roads, byways and some 'roads used as public paths'

The New Access Rights
Access Land

As well as being able to walk on existing rights of way, under the new legislation you now have access to large areas of open land. You can of course continue to use rights of way footpaths to cross this land, but the main difference is that you can now lawfully leave the path and wander at will, but only in areas designated as access land.

Where to Walk

Areas now covered by the new access rights – Access Land – are shown on Ordnance Survey Explorer maps bearing the access land symbol on the front cover.

'Access Land' is shown on Ordnance Survey maps by a light yellow tint surrounded by a pale orange border. New orange coloured 'i' symbols on the maps will show the location of permanent access information boards installed by the access authorities.

Restrictions

The right to walk on access land may lawfully be restricted by landowners. Landowners can, for any reason, restrict access for up to 28 days in any year. They cannot however close the land:

- on bank holidays;
- for more than four Saturdays and Sundays in a year;

- on any Saturday from 1 June to 11 August; or
- on any Sunday from 1 June to the end of September.

They have to provide local authorities with five working days' notice before the date of closure unless the land involved is an area of less than five hectares or the closure is for less than four hours. In these cases land-owners only need to provide two hours' notice.

Whatever restrictions are put into place on access land they have no effect on existing rights of way, and you can continue to walk on them.

Dogs

Dogs can be taken on access land, but must be kept on leads of two metres or less between 1 March and 31 July, and at all times where they are near livestock. In addition landowners may impose a ban on all dogs from fields where lambing takes place for up to six weeks in any year. Dogs may be banned from moorland used for grouse shooting and breeding for up to five years.

In the main, walkers following the routes in this book will continue to follow existing rights of way, but a knowledge and understanding of the law as it affects walkers, plus the ability to distinguish access land marked on the maps, will enable anyone who wishes to depart from paths that cross access land either to take a shortcut, to enjoy a view or to explore.

General Obstructions

Obstructions can sometimes cause a problem on a walk and the most common of these is where the path across a field has been ploughed over. It is legal for a farmer to plough up a path provided that it is restored within two weeks. This does not always happen and you are faced with the dilemma of following the line of the path, even if this means treading on crops, or walking round the edge of the field. Although the later course of action seems the most sensible, it does mean that you would be trespassing.

Other obstructions can vary from overhanging vegetation to wire fences across the path, locked gates or even a cattle feeder on the path.

Use common sense. If you can get round the obstruction without causing damage, do so. Otherwise only remove as much of the obstruction as is necessary to secure passage.

If the right of way is blocked and cannot be followed, there is a long-standing view that in such circumstances there is a right to deviate, but this cannot wholly be relied on. Although it is accepted in law that highways (and that includes rights of way) are for the public service, and if the usual track is impassable, it is for the general good that people should be entitled to pass into another line. However, this should not be taken as indicating a right to deviate whenever a way becomes impassable. If in doubt, retreat.

Report obstructions to the local authority and/or the Ramblers' Association.

Useful Organisations

Council for National Parks
6/7 Barnard Mews, London SW11 1QU
Tel. 020 7924 4077
www.cnp.org.uk

Council for the Protection of Rural England (CPRE)
128 Southwark Street, London SE1 0SW
Tel. 020 7981 2800
www.cpre.org.uk

Cumbria Tourist Board
Ashleigh, Holly Road, Bowness-on-Windermere, Cumbria LA23 2AQ
Tel. 015394 44444
www.golakes.co.uk

Friends of the Lake District
Murley Moss, Oxenholme Road, Kendal, Cumbria LA9 7SS
Tel. 01539 720788
www.fld.org.uk

Lake District National Park Authority information centres *(*not open all year)*:
*Ambleside: 015394 32729

*Bowness Bay: 015394 42895
*Broughton-in-Furness: 01229 716115
*Coniston: 015394 41533
*Glenridding: 017684 82414
*Grasmere: 015394 35245
*Hawkshead: 015394 36525
Keswick: 017687 72645
*Pooley Bridge: 017684 86530
*Waterhead: 015394 32729

Lake District National Park Visitor Centre
Brockhole, Windermere, Cumbria LA23 1LJ
Tel. 015394 46601
www.lake-district.gov.uk

Long Distance Walkers' Association
www.ldwa.org.uk

Muncaster Castle
Open from March to November (except
Saturdays). Reduced rate tickets for walkers
who want to explore the grounds are
usually available at any ticket office
Tel. 01229 717 614 in advance
www.muncaster.co.uk

National Trust
Membership and general enquiries:
PO Box 39, Warrington, WA5 7WD
Tel. 0870 458 4000
North West Regional Office:
The Hollens, Grasmere, Ambleside,
Cumbria LA22 9QZ
Tel. 08706 095391
www.nationaltrust.org.uk

Natural England
1 East Parade, Sheffield, S1 2ET
Tel. 0114 241 8920
www.naturalengland.org.uk

Ordnance Survey
Romsey Road, Maybush,
Southampton SO16 4GU
Tel. 08456 05 05 05 (Lo-call)
www.ordnancesurvey.co.uk

Ramblers' Association
2nd Floor, Camelford House, 87–90
Albert Embankment, London SE1 7TW
Tel. 020 7339 8500
www.ramblers.org.uk

The Ruskin Museum
Open daily all year, (reduced opening
times in winter) Tel. 015394 41164
www.ruskinmuseum.com

Youth Hostels Association
Trevelyan House, Dimple Road,
Matlock, Derbyshire DE4 3YH
Tel. 01629 592600
www.yha.org.uk

 *Ordnance Survey maps of the
Lake District*
The Lake District is covered by Ordnance
Survey 1:50 000 (1¼ inches to 1 mile or
2cm to 1km) scale Landranger map sheets
85, 86, 89, 90, 91, 96, 97 and 98. These
all-purpose maps are packed with
information to help you explore the area.
Viewpoints, picnic sites, places of interest
and caravan and camping sites are shown,
as well as public rights of way information
such as footpaths and bridleways.

To examine the Lake District in more
detail, and especially if you are planning
walks, Ordnance Survey Explorer maps at
1:25 000 (2½ inches to 1 mile or 4cm to
1km) scale are ideal. Four such maps cover
the main Lake District National Park:

OL4 (The English Lakes –
       North-western area)
OL5 (The English Lakes –
       North-eastern area)
OL6 (The English Lakes –
       South-western area)
OL7 (The English Lakes –
       South-eastern area)

The Lake District area is also covered by
Ordnance Survey touring map number 3,
at 1 inch to 1½ miles or 1cm to 1km
(1:100 000) scale, which includes useful
guide information on the reverse.

To get to the Lake District, use the
Ordnance Survey Travel Map-Route at
1:625 000 (1 inch to 10 miles or 4cm to
25km) scale or OS Travel Map-Road 4
(Northern England) at 1:250 000 (1 inch to
4 miles or 1cm to 2.5km) scale.

Ordnance Survey maps and guides are
available from most booksellers, stationers
and newsagents.